Awaiting GOD'S Greatest Gift

Stories, Reflections and Activities Celebrating the Meaning of Christmas

Inspired by Faith

Awaiting God's Greatest Gift
ISBN 978-0-9895802-4-3
Published by Product Concept Mfg., Inc.
2175 N. Academy Circle #200, Colorado Springs, CO 80909

Written and Compiled by Cathy Atkinson, including guest authors in association with Product Concept Mfg., Inc.

All scripture quotations are from the King James version of the Bible unless otherwise noted.

Sayings not having a credit listed are contributed by writers for Product Concept Mfg., Inc. or in a rare case, the author is unknown.

Christmas is surely the most exciting time of the year! There is so much to look forward to, and at the center of it all is the miracle of a Baby who would change the world forever. That is what the Advent season is all about.

On the first day of December, gather your family around and hear a story that tells about the Advent tradition. And don't forget to open window number 1 on your Advent calendar, which follows this page!

Then count down the days until Christmas comes! For 25 days, find time to read the inspiration for that day provided through Scriptures, reflections, legends, poems, songs and stories, many of which are based on true events. An activity is suggested each day, too, giving the family an idea to spend time together in ways that are both meaningful and fun. Most require little preparation, but glance through the book first, so you can have the things you need available.

Christmas will be here before you know it, and your hearts will be ready as you celebrate the real reason for this wonderful season.

DECEMBER

1

We stand, and rejoice in the hope of the glory of God.

Romans 5:2

There is nothing quite as exciting as knowing Christmas is almost here, but, oh my, we have a lot to do! The month before Christmas is called "Advent" because advent means coming; when we think of the words "coming" and "Christmas" together, we think of Jesus. With so many things happening in December, it's easy to get caught up in all the activities and forget why we're celebrating in the first place. Advent gives us a way to be intentional about keeping our focus on Jesus. This Christmas we need to remember that if God had not sent His Son, Jesus, as a baby, and if he hadn't actually been born in a manger that day in Bethlehem, we wouldn't be having a holiday at all. He's the whole reason why we celebrate Christmas!

Creating a family Advent wreath is the perfect way to begin this wonderful season. The best part is there is no one "right" way to construct your wreath! It can be very individual and unique, as simple or as ornate as your family would like. You will need five dripless candles, some type of wreath, or materials to make one, and some pine boughs or decorations.

To create your wreath, use your imagination! You might start with a straw, styrofoam, or grapevine form purchased at a craft store, or use any found materials that can be shaped into a wreath. Then, decorate your wreath base. Many people use pine boughs, but your family can decided what they'd like. When you've finished decorating the base, spray it with a fire-retardant. Lay the wreath flat on a table or display area and then place the candles evenly around the (as in the picture on page 3). You might need to carve out space in the styrofoam, wedge them in, glue them in, or use a small votive holder.

DECEMBER 1

THE KEY

Finding The Real Meaning of Christmas

by Sue Englert

We found it in the attic on the Saturday after Thanksgiving. My brother and I were up there looking for stuff that we could use in the show we always performed for our parents and grandparents on Christmas Eve. We used to use stuffed animals, blankets, and the family dog to act out the Nativity. Now that we're teenagers, it's more of a comedy show with both of us competing for laughter and applause.

Anyway, we always start looking for inspiration in the attic—the place where everything goes that doesn't have any place else to go. There are crates of our baby stuff that Momma is saving for grand-kids "someday," bags of Momma's and Daddy's old clothes, and antiques that Grandma just can't part with.

And there is the mysterious trunk that is locked because Grandma and Grandpa can't remember what they did with the key. It looks like a pirate's treasure chest. We used to imagine that it was filled with gold and that some pirate out there was still searching for it, never knowing that it was right here in North Carolina in our attic. Grandma and Grandpa just laughed when we talked about it, and told us it contained only memories. Whatever the old trunk contained, we never knew because of the mystery of the lost key.

As my brother was modeling Daddy's old pair of bell-bottom pants, a silky shirt with big, pointy collars, and platform shoes (don't ask me, ask my dad), I looked through some of Momma's old clothes that finally fit me. I pulled a big, floppy hat out of one of the boxes and put it on my head. My brother reached over to try to take the hat, and as I dodged his attempted grab, I fell into an old armchair. Instead of saving me, it fell over backward with me in it. We were both laughing hysterically when my brother tried to help me. He reached down to pull me up and said, "Hey, look! There's an old key on the floor! It must have been stuck down behind the chair cushion!" I picked up the beautiful old brass key as we looked at each other and said, "The trunk!"

We worked our way through the attic maze to the trunk. We kneeled down in front of it and put the key in the lock. As I turned the key, we heard a click, and the latch popped loose. We looked at each other, wide-eyed, and opened the trunk. There were stacks of very old scrapbooks, and on top was a contraption that neither of us could identify.

It was a big, dark-colored ring, about the size of a dinner plate—actually two dark metal rings, one a little bit smaller than the other, and they were connected in four places by flat squares of metal with tiny round metal cups on top. When I tried to pick it up, it was much heavier than I thought it would be. My brother carefully lifted it out of the trunk and set it in the chair. We lifted the first of the scrapbooks out, sat down side by side, and opened the book to discover pages and pages of old photographs that were kind of a brownish color and white. As we slowly turned the pages, wondering who the people in the pictures were, we came to a page with a portrait of a girl about my age, looking back at us with big, dark eyes, dark hair, and dimples, just like me. "I wonder who that is," I said softly.

"I don't know," answered my brother, "but she looks a lot like you." It gave me chills.

From downstairs, we heard Momma say, "Are you two still up in the attic? It's time for supper."

"Momma," I shouted, "You won't believe what

we found!" We carried our treasures to the kitchen and laid them on the table.

Momma laughed as we modeled our fashion finds. When she saw the album, she quietly said, "Oh my," and started gently turning the pages. When she got to the picture of the girl, I asked her who it was, and she said, "That's your great-grandmother, Laura, when she was about your age. You look exactly like her!"

My brother picked up the round metal contraption and asked Momma what it was. She said, "I'm going to let Grandma tell you about that." My brother and I just shrugged our shoulders at each other and cleared the table for dinner.

Later, Grandma and Grandpa came over and my brother set the round metal object in front of Grandma. She gasped and exclaimed, "Where on earth did you find this?" My brother pulled the old key from his pocket and we excitedly explained how we found it and opened the old trunk.

Grandma tearfully explained, "This is my grandmother's Advent wreath that she brought with her from Germany. It had been in her family for years. She used it every Christmas, then my mother used it, then I used it. After we moved here to be closer to you, I couldn't find it with my Christmas decorations. I forgot all about it until just now when you set it in front of me."

My brother said the only Advent wreaths he had ever seen were all made of fake stuff—plastic pine branches, poinsettias, or holly. Grandma explained that people used to start with a heavy, iron frame. They would gather real pine boughs and pine cones from the woods, and then arrange them on the round frame. They would put candles in the four candle holders—three purple candles and one special pink candle. She told us how it was the official start of the countdown to Jesus's birth, and it was very exciting to light the candles, adding one on each of the four Sundays leading up to Christmas. When the special pink candle was lighted on the last Sunday before Christmas, it was magical.

After Grandma explained the tradition, I asked her if we could start it again, using the antique Advent wreath. She fought back tears as she nodded and said, "Of course we can. Let's assemble the wreath and light the first candle tomorrow after church. It will be our tradition now, and you can carry it on with your children and grandchildren—as long as you can remember where you put the wreath and you don't lose the key."

DECEMBER 2

God sent the angel Gabriel
to Nazareth, a town in Galilee,
to a virgin pledged to be married
to a man named Joseph...
The virgin's name was Mary.

Luke 1:26–27 NIV

Nazareth wasn't a very big town. But it was home for both Mary and Joseph. They weren't important leaders in their city; they weren't a prince and princess, they didn't have a lot of money or power or beauty. But God knew Mary and Joseph were two people who loved Him and loved each other. He knew they would serve Him faithfully. And God chose the small town of Nazareth as the place that Jesus would call home.

December 2

God has a plan for each of us and He isn't waiting for us to be the smartest or funniest, prettiest or most successful person before He loves us. He loves us right now, just the way we are. We might live in a small town in the middle of nowhere or in a small apartment in the middle of a huge city, but those things aren't important to God. What matters is that we love Him and that we are faithful to Him.

Most of us know men and women serving in the military. These men and women are so brave! Whether they are in the midst of front-line battles or serving stateside, each one is providing an invaluable service to our country. Everyone in the military has had moments where they feel alone. They not only risk their lives for our country's freedom, they often must sacrifice special holiday time with their own family.

Take some time together as a family to bake cookies, brownies, or a loaf of banana bread and write a quick note of appreciation to someone in the military. Ask each family member to write a note or draw a picture. Let your new friend know that your family is praying for him or her. This is something tangible we can do for someone who might be alone this holiday.

DECEMBER 2

HOME FOR CHRISTMAS

by Laurie Harper

Christmas was only weeks away but you would have never known it by the looks of Steve and Cathy's house. They didn't even have a Christmas tree! Their only child was in the military and not coming home for Christmas, so no one was in the mood for decorating the house this year.

Steve and Cathy knew their son, Ryan, was doing what he always wanted to do, flying planes for the Air Force. He was stationed in Japan and being so far away from home, an occasional phone call or letter was the only communication they had with him. It had been a year since he left for Japan and it didn't sound like he would be coming home any time soon. Even though he wasn't home for any of the other holidays, not being home for Christmas was going to be hard.

The phone rang and Cathy was pleasantly surprised to hear Ryan on the other end. "Hi Mom, are you making those good Christmas cookies yet?" Cathy smiled as she was thought of the times she had to hide the cookies so Ryan and Steve wouldn't eat them all. "No, not yet," Cathy replied. The truth was she wasn't in the Christmas spirit to do anything. Ryan told her he sure wished he could be home for Christmas but there was another guy in his squadron that was married with children and Ryan thought it was more important for him to get home for Christmas. Someone had to stay on base, and it looked like Ryan would be the one. Of course Cathy understood and felt proud once again that her son was so sensitive and thoughtful, but she couldn't help but feel an emptiness. Ryan told her to get busy, he wanted some of those cookies mailed to him! That was all Cathy needed to hear to give her a good reason to start baking. Six dozen cookies later, she was in the basement trying to find a suitable box to pack them in when Steve came home. Cathy fought back the tears as she told Steve about the phone call from Ryan and how the little glimmer of hope that he might be home for Christmas was finally gone. They both hugged each other and even Steve had to wipe away a tear.

Christmas Eve finally arrived and they went to the service at church, as usual. Driving home afterward, they noticed, as they got closer to their block, that people were standing outside their house. As they pulled up to the house, the people started cheering, and their neighbor, Rick, hurried them from the car and told them they needed to come stand in front of their house. As they stood watching in dismay, Rick's wife, Sally, pulled up in the driveway, got out of the car, and opened the passenger door. There, dressed in his Air Force uniform, stood Ryan. Everyone cheered as Cathy ran into the arms of her son. "But how did this happen?,"Cathy asked, "How were you able to come home?" Ryan explained that their commander had been able to switch things around so more people were able to be home for Christmas.

DECEMBER 2

As the neighbors said their goodbyes, and Steve, Cathy and Ryan made their way inside, Ryan noticed right away that there was not the usual overload of Christmas decorations in every corner of the house. In fact, there wasn't even a tree! "What's going on here?," he asked. "I know I always give you a hard time about overdoing the decorating, but you don't even have a tree." Cathy admitteed that the idea of being without him for Christmas just took away their joy for the season.

"Hey, let's sit for awhile," Ryan said as he lead his parents to the familiar kitchen table. "It's hard to be away from family at Christmas, but for so many folks, that's a reality they have to live with. You always taught me about the real spirit of Christmas." He glanced in to the living room at the empty space where the Christmas tree lights normally lit up the window. "And Mom, Dad, the world sure needs more light."

His parents nodded, so proud of their son. They realized the roles had shifted and now Ryan was the one who was doing the teaching. "Son, want to give us a hand in the basement?," Steve asked. "We only have a few hours before Christmas to get this place decorated."

"Sure," Ryan said, "but first..." He looked all around the kitchen. "Have any of those cookies?"

DECEMBER 3

...the angel said to her,
"Do not be afraid, Mary...
You will...give birth to a son,
and you are to call him Jesus.

Luke 1:30–31 NIV

Have you ever seen an angel? Many people tell of experiences they have had of seeing and talking with them. Sometimes people know when an angel has appeared to them, but sometimes an angel might not look like we expect and so we may not realize it's an angel. We don't know much about angels. But two things we do know: angels are sent from God, and they come with a message of love.

In the Bible God sent an angel named Gabriel to let Mary know she was going to have a baby. It must have really startled her when Gabriel appeared. But he didn't want her to be afraid. Then he told her the Good news, the plan to send God's Son, Jesus, to be born here on earth. "What do you mean? How can it happen?" she asked him. She loved God and wanted to honor Him. Whatever Gabriel was telling her to do, she would do it.

We might not understand what it is that God has planned, but we can decide to follow Him no matter what. God sent an angel to tell Mary about His plan. But even before the angel came, Mary was ready to serve God. Are you ready to serve God? When you seek Him, you will be blessed beyond imagination. And don't be surprised if you see an angel!

Be an "Angel Family" for someone or for another family in your church or community. Each time you go to the grocery store, pick up extra non–perishable foods and set them aside in a box. When you have filled the box, have everyone sign a card, "From Your Angel Family", and deliver it anonymously.

SEND ME A MIRACLE

By Dorie Allington

"Are you out there, God?," Eli yelled into the dark snowy sky. He had been shaken to the core by a series of disappointments that left him in despair. College had not worked out for him, he had no job and was losing his place to stay just before Christmas. Most of all, he was losing his sense of purpose. And then there was Emmy. She had started out as a great friend and he began to wonder if the feelings could grow into something more. She generously helped him with his studies, but when she suggested he could apply himself more, he responded badly, hurting her feelings, and he just let her go. He felt he had nothing left. "If you're really there, God, show me. I need a miracle. A big one." He felt everything, including his faith, was hanging by a very thin thread.

He was standing on a downtown rooftop, not even remembering exactly how he'd ended up there after walking for hours through the night. Now just before the new day broke, he saw a star still shining through the snow, twinkling. Maybe it was a message! "Nah, that's not going to do it, God. I need a real miracle."

A small grey bird lighted on the railing within inches of his hand. It cocked its head and looked up at the young man, who stared back and waited. "Well, if you're going to start speaking to me, maybe I'll believe...otherwise, you're just a bird, not a miracle." The bird flew away. Frustrated, angry, Eli kicked at the roof, sending a chunk of rubble off the edge.

"Hey, who's up there?!," a voice called up. And not a happy one. Eli peered over the railing and saw on the sidewalk below, a very grumpy looking older woman glaring up at him. She stood beside an open box of baked goods...with a chunk of rubble on top. "I'm calling the police right now unless you come down here." How could things get worse?

Eli found the fire escape he had climbed up earli–er and made his way down to face the consequences of his actions...better to deal with this cranky old woman than the cops.

The tongue–lashing lecture she gave him seemed to go on longer than his college lectures, but finally she simmered down when he said he'd work off the damage: two squashed bread loaves and a ruined pie. In his heart, Eli knew he'd done a very careless thing. What if the rubble had hit the lady?

She had no trouble coming up with ways for him to work off his mistake. She showed him a narrow staircase which led to a room upstairs. It had clearly been an office, with a couch, desk and an old typewriter.

It also housed stacks of boxes and supplies. He was to carry down boxes while she stood at the bottom step, describing what she wanted. He did as he was told. There was a grimy window in the room and while catching his breath, he wiped an area clean with an old rag and caught his breath at the scene outside. The grey storm seemed to be lifting and the snow was sparkling white under the golden sun. He was also surprised by all the dust he saw dancing around through that stream of light. Apparently no one had climbed those stairs in a while because the place was a dusty mess.

Eli had no idea how much time had passed when all the required boxes were finally downstairs. What he did know was that he was dirty, his muscles were sore, his body was tired, and that it felt...really good! The old lady, who had told him to call her May, looked much softer now and invited him to sit behind the counter with her where she put a plate of cakes in front of him. He suddenly realized how ravenous he felt.

"I don't know why you did such a foolish thing," she told him, "but you've made it right," she started out. "Now I have something to ask you. I can't do all the things I used to. Obviously I can't lift all those heavy boxes and I have a very hard time with those stairs. I can't offer you a great big salary or anything, but if you want to work for me, I can pay you modestly. And if by any chance you need a place to stay, you could fix that room upstairs."

Eli couldn't speak. Instead, he just nodded his head. May smiled and then tears glistened in her blue eyes. "Eli, I wasn't sure I could go on here and I was about to give up. Just this morning I asked God to show me what to do and if He intended for me to carry on, to send me a miracle. This may sound silly, but I believe He sent you to me. Do you believe in miracles?"

Eli was barely able to get the answer out: "Yes, I do."

He felt full, refreshed, and ready to get back to work. But first he went up to his new room where he sat at the desk, placed a piece of paper in the type-writer and began:

"Dear Emmy..."

DECEMBER

4

And Mary said:
"My soul glorifies the Lord
and my spirit rejoices in God my Savior..."

Luke 1:46–47 NIV

Mary's whole life had just been turned upside down. She might have felt that she had good reason to be worried and fearful. She was young and engaged to Joseph when she received the message from the angel, Gabriel. She was going to give birth to God's Son. How could that be? Mary had a choice: she could panic about what to do and who to tell and how she should handle the scandal that was about to hit the daily news. Or, Mary could keep trusting God as she had been all along, knowing that He would make His plan clear and that she was simply to follow Him.

Mary's heart was full of praises for God. Her song of praise in Luke 1 reveals a heart bursting with joy, humbled and amazed. God loves it when we sing. Music is an expression of the joy we feel inside; the peace and the overwhelming gratefulness we have toward God easily finds expression in song. Mary couldn't help but sing a song of praise, and we find ourselves, too, singing songs of joy and praise at Christmastime.

Enjoy a night of music and laughter with your loved ones! Have everyone secretly write the name of a Christmas song on a piece of paper and place them in a bowl. Take turns drawing a song title out. See who can "name the tune" when you hum or play the melody on a kazoo. It's not always as easy as it sounds. You can even bring out some impromptu musical instruments: rice in a jar or an overturned box for percussion, a paper towel tube for a horn. It's sure to bring merriment to your time together.

SILENT NIGHT

by Patricia Mitchell

Many stories surround the origin of the beloved hymn, *Silent Night.* Though many details are long lost to history, we know that the carol's words were composed around 1816 by Joseph Mohr, an Austrian pastor. Perhaps the inspiration for the words came to him as he looked upon the stillness of a field blanketed in newly fallen snow...in the tranquility of a village showered in glimmering starlight...or by the anticipation of hearing, once again, the story of the Babe in the manger.

On Christmas Eve day two years later, Mohr took the words of *Silent Night* to his friend, Franz Gruber, a musician, and requested a singable, guitar-friendly tune for the poem. Why guitar? Some say because mice had eaten the bellows of the organ church...others that the organ was broken...still others that Mohr simply liked guitar music. Whatever the reason, the melody was ready by that very evening, in time for the midnight service.

Stille Nacht! Heilige Nacht! debuted in the little village church of Oberndorf, Austria, and from there the hymn has won the hearts of people throughout the world. It has been translated in numerous languages, and its evocative tune is universally recognized.

DECEMBER 4

SILENT NIGHT, HOLY NIGHT

Silent night, holy night,
All is calm, all is bright,
'Round yon virgin Mother and Child,
Holy infant so tender and mild,
Sleep in heavenly peace,
Sleep in heavenly peace.

Silent night, holy night,
Shepherds quake at the sight,
Glories stream from heaven afar,
Heavenly hosts sing Alleluia;
Christ the Savior is born,
Christ the Savior is born.

Silent night, holy night,
Son of God, love's pure light,
Radiant beams from Thy holy face,
With the dawn of redeeming grace,
Jesus, Lord, at Thy birth,
Jesus, Lord, at Thy birth!

Tune: Franz Xaver Gruber, 1818
Text: Joseph Mohr, 1816
Translation: John Freeman Young, 1863

All is Calm...

On December 24, 1914, what would later become known as World War I was in its fourth month. British and French troops were, like their German counterparts, hunkered down in cold, rain-soaked trenches with a short no-man's land between them.

As the day wore on, gunfire tapered off, and finally ceased as evening drew near. Then from the German trenches, the uneasy silence was lifted with the voices of men softly singing in the twilight...*Stille Nacht... Heilige Nacht*...like gentle threads of peace, the familiar carol reached across no-man's land. After a few minutes, voices drifted up from British and French trenches, weaving a tapestry of true, heartfelt peace...*silent night... holy night...sainte nuit...belle nuit...*

One by one, men from both sides climbed out of their trenches and joined on no-man's land, exchanging what small gifts they had to offer. On Christmas Day, the troops shared meals, sang songs, and teamed up to play a make-shift game of soccer. In some places along enemy lines, guns lay silent through New Year's Day.

During a horrific period of war, the impromptu Christmas Truce—brought on by a carol with the power to touch the hearts of every nation—remains one of the most unusual interludes in Western history.

DECEMBER

5

...the angel of the LORD appeared unto him in a dream, saying, Joseph, thou son of David, fear not to take unto thee Mary thy wife...

Matthew 1:20

Joseph was in a tough position. He loved Mary and wanted to protect her. He also wanted to obey God's rules. He may have been frustrated or confused by what was happening, but God chose Joseph as Jesus' earthly father. Why? What did God see in Joseph?

Joseph was a man of integrity. That means he kept his promises, was hard–working and honest, humble and kind. He was willing to put Mary's feelings and needs ahead of his own, and keep his commitment to her because he trusted God. When the angel appeared to Joseph in a dream, he took it seriously. He obeyed God even though he didn't know what the outcome would be.

Sometimes things don't turn out the way we thought they would, even though we have been trusting God and living our lives for Him. Sometimes God allows us to be in tough situations so we have a chance to hold on tight to His hand. God wants us to trust Him no matter what, just like Joseph and Mary did.

Plan a fun night out on the town with your family. Each person should suggest what they'd like to do: Attend a Christmas concert or Nativity play? See a just-released Christmas movie? Go to a nice restaurant for scrumptious desserts? Then talk about the choices and come to a decision that everyone feels good about.

Families make compromises for each other—isn't that what Mary and Joseph did? Our actions and attitudes, compromises and decisions as a family can show this type of integrity as well. Try to make time for your family to talk about what you have just seen or experienced, and what your expectations were. What about our expectations of Christmas? How can we keep our focus on Jesus in spite of all the hype?

December 5

A Story Of Hope And Faith

by Laurie Harper

Typically with only a few weeks before Christmas, I am crossing off the days on the calendar and dreaming of all the gifts under the tree for me. But this year was different. Dad lost his job a month ago, and even though Mom worked, there was not enough money for anything extra.

Mom was trying to get my brother, Mark, and me off to church for our Christmas program rehearsal but I didn't even want to go because I usually got a beautiful new dress for the program and I knew that wasn't going to happen this year. This was just going to be an awful Christmas and I didn't even want to be in the church program. As I threw my tantrum of what an awful year this was, Mom quietly sat me down and reminded me that Christmas should not be about the gifts, new dress, or anything material. I was forgetting the true meaning of Christmas and needed to change my attitude. I hated it when Mom was right, but she was, so I dragged myself to the rehearsal.

As I lay in bed feeling completely sorry for myself, Mark knocked on my bedroom door. He told me he was thinking about a Christmas gift for Mom and Dad and said he'd been talking to Mr. Carlson, our neighbor.

First of all, I couldn't believe he would even go near his house and then actually talk to Mr. Carlson, also known to everyone on the block as Mr. Crabby! Even Mom called him Mr. Crabby. Mark said he asked him if he had any odd jobs he and I could do for him to earn some money to buy our parents a Christmas present. Mark said as he was coming home from school today, Mr. Carlson flagged him over to the house and told him he had thought about it and he'd like me to do some housecleaning and Mark could scoop the snow off his driveway. He'd pay us each $20.

I never saw Mr. Crabby smile and he even smelled old. But, knowing I only had $2.46 to my name, I didn't have much choice. Mark said we'd go over to his house on Saturday. Much to my surprise, his house was quite nice inside but it did smell like old Mr. Crabby. We did our work and as he paid us, Mark thanked him and told him we were going to get a new toaster oven for Mom and Dad with the money for Christmas. I think he gave us a grumpy approval.

Mom gave us the final 30 minute warning before leaving for Christmas Eve church and the dreaded program. I left the house wearing the same old dress I wore last year but Mom did give me one of her necklaces to wear, and it must have made it look different because several friends gave me compliments. I was pleasantly surprised that wearing a repeat Christmas dress wasn't the end of the world.

Christmas morning was finally here and Mark and I ran downstairs to the Christmas tree as we traditionally did. We just stood there as we saw only three gifts under the tree, with the biggest one being the toaster oven from Mark and me. We tried not to act disappointed but Mom and Dad quickly asked us to sit down. They reminded us about the tight budget and thanked us for being so understanding. They each handed us our small package and said we had to open it at the same time.

As we opened the gifts, Dad slipped out of the room. Mark and I looked at each other as we each held a can of cat food. Before we could say anything Dad came in the room with a box. As he put the box under the tree, two small kittens tried to get out of the box. "Merry Christmas" shouted Mom and Dad! Mark and I screamed with delight. We decided to name our new kittens Hope and Faith. What I thought was going to be the worst Christmas was actually the very best.

DECEMBER

6

And it came to pass in those days, that there went out a decree from Caesar Augustus that all the world should be taxed.
And Joseph also went up from Galilee, out of the city of Nazareth, into Judaea, unto the city of David, which is called Bethlehem;
To be taxed with Mary his espoused wife, being great with child.

Luke 2:2,4-5

Talk about terrible timing! Mary was nine months pregnant when she and Joseph had to travel to Bethlehem, the city of their ancestors. Bethlehem was a long way from Nazareth, and Mary and Joseph would have to walk or ride a donkey to get there. That meant at least a week of traveling, following dusty trails by day and sleeping on the rocky ground at night. Poor Mary! Riding on the bumpy back of a donkey all day long, every day for a week had to be miserable. She must have been very tired and uncomfortable by the time they finally got to Bethlehem.

Mary and Joseph were not the only ones traveling to Bethlehem for the census. Many, many people had crowded into the little town. So many people were there that when Mary and Joseph arrived, they couldn't find anywhere to stay for the night. What were they going to do? Mary knew the time for the baby to be born was very close. Where could they go?

Invite someone who will be alone for Christmas to share the day (or evening) with your family. This is such a simple gesture it often gets overlooked. Or we think that someone else has already asked them, or that it will take away from our own family time, or maybe they won't want to come.

Honestly, if you really think about it, isn't this the very heart of what loving God is all about? We show our love for Him by loving His children, by sharing our lives with others. An invitation to Christmas dinner, playing games and swapping stories could brighten up a lonely heart. Your life is worth sharing and you can make a difference in someone else's life.

THE LONG LANE LEADING HOME

By Doris Carter Wardlow

I was a sad and lonely teenager that Christmas. Oh, we did the best we could, Daddy and Mom and me, but our country was at war and in the midst of its battles were our friends, our neighbors, and these four: all three of my brothers and my sweetheart. Even in a small rural area like ours, there was not a household that Christmas that was not touched in some way by the war's grip.

We made cookies to send across the ocean. Mom sewed the panels to hang in our window, signifying we had someone serving our country. The panel had three blue stars, one for each son. We prayed none would turn to gold, the symbol of a family member who died in battle. We brought soldiers from the Army training camp an hour away to come spend weekends with us at our farm. I played piano and sang for them, my mom made wonderful country meals for them, and we took them to church with us (not asking them what their religious preferences were). And all the while, we prayed. And prayed. We prayed for our boys to be safe, and that someone would care for them that Christmas.

DECEMBER 6

It took a long time for a letter to come from overseas and we never knew when to expect one. Our mailman, knowing how anxiously we awaited word, would turn off the main road onto our lane, and drive all the way up to the house, honking the horn the whole way. A letter from one of our sailors! And that is how we learned that prayers had been answered, for one by one, my sweetheart, youngest brother, and middle brother, all let us know they would be settled in another country this holiday, but would be out of the battle lines. If only we would hear from Kenneth, my oldest brother and the one who was on a ship in the grips of battle in the Pacific Ocean.

We put up a big cedar tree which my dad had cut from the grove, and put a few ornaments on it, and by this time we had electricity in the house and had a string of lights. I determined that we were going to leave those lights on every night to welcome Kenneth home...when he came. I prayed desperately that he would. The bulbs did not last that long, though, and we did not have replacements. They would have a metal tip and metal was rationed as it was required for the war effort. I figured out that when a bulb burned out, I could put tin foil behind it and the lights would stay lit by bypassing the bad bulb. Daddy was a farmer but also had learned to do electrical work as electricity came to our part of the country. He must have cringed at my methods but he knew how important this symbol was to me, and he allowed me to do it. But time went by and the lights began to go out.

A scream came from behind our house, so loud it was heard by those on neighboring farms. Daddy was nearly a mile away clearing brush and he came running. I had never heard that sound before, and came running around the house to see that it was Mom in the garden where she had been doing late clean–up, and where now she was yelling and running toward the lane. She had been the first to see the bus pull up off the main road, where a Sailor boy got off and began walking the long lane up to our house. Only three bulbs were left burning on the tree by then on that evening. My brother, Kenneth, was home.

DECEMBER 7

And she brought forth her firstborn son, and wrapped him in swaddling clothes, and laid him in a manger...

Luke 2:7

A new baby is certainly a cause for wonder. For nine long months we wait and pray and look forward to the arrival of this tiny life. When the day finally arrives, we can hardly contain our excitement. We want to hold him, to touch his curled up fingers and rosebud lips. He is absolutely beautiful. The excitement spills over from the parents to grandparents, aunts, uncles, cousins, neighbors and friends—no one is immune to the joy when a new baby is born.

That's because it is a miracle. Every single baby is born because of the touch of God's hand. It was

God that formed that little one; none of us could do anything but watch. He made the little face and the tiny fingers, the ears and decided on the shape of the nose. We stood by and looked at the pictures. God decided boy or girl, blue eyes or brown or green or black. He put the tiny dimples on or left them off and chose all manner of skin and hair colors. We did none of that. It was all God. The next time you get to hold a newborn, think about how incredible it really is that this new life was formed by the God of the Universe.

The special birthday we await is a time to be mindful of the babies in the world who have little, just like Baby Jesus, who slept in a manger instead of a crib, and was covered in cloths instead of nice clothes. Invite friends young and old to join you for a "baby shower" for children in need. Suggest they bring either an unwrapped plush toy animal, cozy baby blanket, or baby clothes. Lay blankets and quilts on the floor and couch for guests to sit on, and make a "manger" to hold the gifts as they arrive. This could be a box, basket or crib. Gather around the manger, with plush animals playing the nativity animals, sing "Away in a Manger" and talk about what it would have been like to be at Jesus' birth. Enjoy looking at all the sweet gifts, then wrap them in tissue paper to deliver to a charity for children in need.

A PRIZE WINNING QUILT

by Cathy Atkinson

The grand prize winning quilt in the Alpine Valley Quilt Show had vanished into thin air, and the entire town of Silver Springs was in an uproar. Police were already going door to door, asking if anyone had information about the missing quilt; Sally Beaufort had called down to The Daily Sentinel and talked to Maye Quintana who said it would run tomorrow morning as a front page article. Nothing much exciting ever happened around Silver Springs, so disappearing quilts warranted a great deal of attention. What made the situation a little more complicated was the fact that it was two days before Christmas.

The police had dispatched Eddie McMillen and Dave Basky to the First Baptist Church where the ladies were frantic, and they showed up, ready to solve the crime and get on with more pressing holiday activities. However, it was beginning to look as if the ladies of the quilting societies had more questions for the police than the police did for them. How in the world could someone break in and steal the quilt right out from under their noses?

The women were livid. This was personal. Annabeth Petrie had spent the better part of a year working on that quilt and no one was going to just waltz in and walk away with it.

This year had been the biggest show they'd ever had with the Southern River Guild bringing in several quilts, a new club that drove down from Barclay entering quilts in several categories, and the biggest club in the state, Mountain Memories, who had quilts in every category. It was so big this year they'd had to move from First Presbyterian where the show had been held for twenty-one years, to the First Baptist Church's Fellowship Hall. They knew they were cutting things close with the city's annual Christmas Pageant being held there the night after the quilt show finals. But they had all agreed to have their quilts and belongings removed from the Fellowship Hall premises by 2:00 this afternoon. That way the City Council members could set up all the chairs and get the tables ready for the Pageant and the Bake Sale Auction.

The Silver Springs Annual Children's Pageant was the kind of thing the entire town showed up for. If you didn't have children or grandchildren in the pageant, your neighbors did, and not a soul in Silver Springs would miss the chance to see their kids in action. Plus, Erma Metsker always brought her famous Double Fudge and Cream Cheese Brownies to auction at the bake sale after the play. You can bet the whole town would be bidding on those brownies.

Every year the pageant was produced, directed and acted out by the children of Silver Springs, with a bit of oversight by Miss Patty Shepherd, the high school drama teacher. Auditions for the coveted main parts were held in late October, giving those kids ample time to practice. The sewing club volunteered to make costume adjustments and city council members helped with the curtains and audience control. The police and fire departments were in charge of ticket sales and collection. It was a whole town affair.

Anyway, back to the quilt. Eddie and Dave took copious notes on this mystifying case. Where was the quilt last seen? Who saw it and at what time? Who would have wanted to steal the quilt and what was the motive? The final judging had taken place last night and when the ladies came to collect their quilts this morning, Annabeth's quilt had simply vanished. Annabeth was, understandably, a wreck. The women looked through all the booths and quilt displays, hoping to find it tucked away somewhere, protected, in a safe place. But the beautiful quilt was nowhere to be found. It was absolutely shocking to think that someone in their small town would be so bold.

With all the careful searching and the questions, they were stumped. Dave and Eddie decided to check back with the Sergeant in case something had turned up in the door-to-door search. But there wasn't a trace of evidence. By 3:00 that afternoon, with nothing yet discovered, the quilt mystery had to be put on the back burner as children began arriving at Fellowship Hall to get ready for the pageant. The council members present were now hustling around getting chairs set up, doing final checks on the lights and placing tables for the Bake Sale goods. The ladies of Silver Springs began bringing in their most delectable and scrumptious desserts, placing each beautiful bowl, plate and pie dish on the tables. Soon the tables were laden with delicacies sure to bring in top dollar for the Town Council's Holiday Slush Fund. Millie Knight's Pecan Pie, Sally Winder's Three Day Coconut Cake and an amazing looking Blueberry Buckle brought in by Suzie Adams were among the first to arrive.

At 6:15, Mayor J.P. Moore checked the microphone, "Testing...one, two, three..." An excited buzz was settling over the growing crowd. People began to take seats, getting video cameras set up on tripods, ready to go. Annabeth Petrie, obviously still shaken, was ushered in by her husband, Joe. They sat down in front because their son, Joe–Joe Jr. had gotten the part of first wise man. Trina Connor and several other members of the Quilting Club sat behind Annabeth just to show their support.

By 7:00 the place was packed, last minute comers were sneaking in the back and trying to find seats. A hush came over the crowd.

Mayor Moore stepped up to the microphone and welcomed everyone to this year's Pageant, and, as he did every year, asked for help taking down the chairs after the Bake Sale Auction was over. Then, it was finally time. The lights went out, a hush came over the crowd and a spotlight appeared on the far left of the stage. Kelly Adams, now dressed as the angel Gabriel, was standing on a stool. The Host of Angels (five of the first graders) stood around her on the stage, each holding a wand with a star on the end, sparkling with gold glitter. "Long, long ago, in the city of Bethlehem, a baby boy was born." Kelly began in her sweet angel voice. The Angels began to sing "O Little Town of Bethlehem," and Phil Adams cued for the curtains to be drawn back.

At that moment a faint gasp could be heard by those sitting in the general area of Annabeth Petrie. All eyes were on center stage where the stable scene was beautifully set. A real live donkey, and three real sheep milled around behind the manger.

Scott Milroy was playing the part of Joseph this year and five year–old Katie Quintana was Mary. They were kneeling on either side of an elaborate manger. I say elaborate because it was probably the nicest manger that a baby Jesus doll has ever had. Draped across that wooden trough, and wrapped around the doll, was Annabeth's prize–winning quilt.

That morning at the dress rehearsal, little Katie had been desperate for some sort of "swaddling" for the doll which had no clothes. She refused to have a naked baby Jesus. The quilt was right there, hanging on the wall, and it was soft and beautiful and perfect. When Katie saw the big blue ribbon, she knew it was a special quilt and must have been made for a very special baby. Katie knew that special baby was Jesus. Breathing a sigh of relief, Annabeth couldn't have agreed more.

REMEMBERING THE GIFT

(based on a poem by Doris Carter Wardlow)

There was a sparkling Christmas tree
Where tinsel glistened joyfully.
Bright garland danced from branch to branch,
And golden bulbs were elegant.
But tucked among the shimmering fare,
A humble figure rested there—
A wooden crib and paper crown
That brought the Christmas message down—
A Baby born one silent night,
God's gift to us of heaven's light.

DECEMBER 8

...there was no room
for them in the inn.

Luke 2:7

There is no hiding true kindness. The Bethlehem innkeeper must have been a very kindhearted man. We don't really know what he was like because he is never actually mentioned in the Bible. But we can guess that someone was in charge that night, and that he didn't have the heart to send Mary and Joseph away. The innkeeper gave them the best place he had available—the stable where he kept his animals.

December 8

It may have been a cave, or it may have been an extra room underneath or next to the main house. I'm sure it didn't matter to Mary at that point. But isn't it interesting to wonder what the innkeeper must have thought as he showed them to the stable. Did he have any clue what God was doing? What did he think when the shepherds came with their sheep? Did he see and hear the angels singing Glory to God in the Highest? Did he recognize that this was the Son of God?

Set up a family-friendly nativity scene or crèche for your family to enjoy. Many families have special, fragile, and heirloom nativity scenes that they like to display at Christmas. This is not that one. This nativity is one that can be handled by any and all family members and visitors, young and old. It is one that should be placed somewhere within reach of family members at all times. It is one that can be well loved over the years and still be loved some more.

By keeping a nativity set available to set up and act out, we become personally involved in the actual events. We act out the angels' announcement to the shepherds on the hillside. We bring the Three Kings in to worship and present gifts. Each event is personalized when we re-create the story this way, and it becomes more real to us, and more fun.

DECEMBER 8

THE LEGEND OF THE LITTLE DONKEY

By Doris Carter Wardlow

On a cold, wintry night in a small town not far from busy Jerusalem, a small donkey wandered into a stable. She had come to get warm. It seemed to be a very crowded place, and a strange group gathered there. She recognized some of the shepherds from the nearby hills, and there were lots of animals—all focused on something.

The donkey pushed her way to the front. She saw a man and a pretty lady, looking adoringly into a manger. The little donkey edged closer and looked over the side of the manger. She saw a tiny, bright-eyed baby looking out at a brand new world. Five wee fingers reached up and touched the donkey's nose. It was the sweetest caress she had ever known. The donkey lay down and knew she never wanted to leave the baby's side.

When it came time for the man and woman and baby to leave, they would not let her follow, because she did not belong to them. Her owner came and took her home with the rest of his flock.

Years passed and the little donkey grew old. She became a mother and a grandmother, and pastured near the Mount of Olives overlooking Jerusalem. She had a feisty grandson who liked to play and buck and have fun all day long. Sometimes, the owner had to tie the colt to settle him down.

One day, two men came to the village. They told the owner, "The Lord has need of your colt." The feisty donkey acted up because he did not want to go. At that moment a man with very kind eyes passed the old donkey and touched her. She recognized that gentle touch: it was the tiny babe from the manger in Bethlehem.

The old donkey called her grandson aside, and in their own language told him he should straighten up because he had been chosen to carry the King.

At once, the feisty little donkey pricked up his ears, held his head high, and straightened his back. He would proudly carry the King of Kings!

–Inspired by the book of Luke, chapters 2 and 19

LUKE 19:29–38 NIV

As [Jesus] approached Bethphage and Bethany at the hill called the Mount of Olives, he sent two of his disciples, saying to them,

"Go to the village ahead of you, and as you enter it, you will find a colt tied there, which no one has ever ridden. Untie it and bring it here.

If anyone asks you, 'Why are you untying it?' say, 'The Lord needs it.'"

Those who were sent ahead went and found it just as he had told them.

As they were untying the colt, its owners asked them, "Why are you untying the colt?"

They replied, "The Lord needs it."

They brought it to Jesus, threw their cloaks on the colt and put Jesus on it.

As he went along, people spread their cloaks on the road.

When he came near the place where the road goes down the Mount of Olives, the whole crowd of disciples began joyfully to praise God in loud voices for all the miracles they had seen:

"Blessed is the king who comes in the name of the Lord!"

DECEMBER 9

The Lord...[says]:
"I have loved you
with an everlasting love..."

Jeremiah 31:3 NIV

Christmas is about love. It's all about God's love for us and our love for Him. Two thousand years ago God's love for us showed up as Jesus in a manger. Our love for Him came through as caring young parents, worshipping shepherds and wise men who followed a shining star. We have always shown our love for God in many different ways. Some people like to sing—like the angels did that night. Some people tell others about Him—

like the shepherds did. Some people give Him gifts—just like the wise men did. However it is you show your love, He accepts your gift. His love for us is everywhere—in the love of our friends, our family, and the joyous celebration of His Son's birth.

Think about someone who has played a very special role in your life. Christmas is the perfect time to do something to show your love and gratitude. Can you take that person out for lunch and spend some time together or send a special Christmas card with a handwritten note? Or take the time for a phone call? It may take time and effort but it's worth it, because by loving others, you get blessings in return. Our love for one another is the best gift we can ever give. Have some fun—who would you like to show love this Christmas season?

PATCHWORK OF OUR PAST

by Cathy Atkinson

My Great-Aunt Anna was a little bit quirky. She lived in a little house in the Southwest desert with my Great-Uncle Fred. Aunt Anna was tall, and wrinkled all over. She wore turquoise and silver jewelry she got from the Native American Indians, and colorful dresses she made with material that looked like the sunset. Her arms were tanned from the desert sun and she smiled as big as a beautiful Indian moon. Aunt Anna loved to sew and her sewing machine sat proudly right in the front room. She always had some sort of sewing project going on, most of the time she made quilts for the kids on the Reservation. I loved to run my fingers through the soft, pretty material she had stacked neatly on the shelf and imagine what I would use it for if I could sew.

Aunt Anna was soft when she hugged me and her arms seemed to wrap around twice as she gathered me up close. And her hugs weren't the quick kind either. Aunt Anna smelled like lavender flowers and she played the piano. My mom said she played with gusto. When I was there she'd scoot over so there was a bit of room for me on the piano bench, and she'd say, "Come sing with me, Cathy." So I'd climb up close to her, and she'd play and we'd sing *Oh, Suzanna,* and *She'll Be Coming 'Round the Mountain,* and *America the Beautiful.* It was ok if I didn't know the words, she sang loud enough for both of us. I loved her. And there was never a doubt in my mind that my Great-Aunt Anna loved me.

We went to see Aunt Anna and Uncle Fred every Christmas and sometimes in-between. Our family of six along with my grandparents and some other relatives would fill their little home right up, but there always seemed to be enough room. We never had much money and we didn't usually have a tree, but we'd decorate the cactus that was in the living room and have Mexican Pie for Christmas dinner. We played Rummy and sang Christmas carols with Aunt Anna accompanying on the piano. If it got claustrophobic in the house, the kids would all head outdoors and play Kick-the-Can in the dirt until the sun went down. It may have been an unconventional sort of Christmas, but we loved it.

On Christmas Eve we were allowed to open two presents, and we always knew ahead of time what they were going to be: we each got a pair of pajamas that Aunt-Anna had made, and we got a

Christmas book from Uncle Fred that we all shared. The best part was that the pajamas always went with the book. Like the year the book was *A Cowboy Christmas,* our pajama material had horses and lariats and horseshoes all over it. And the year we got *The Night Before Christmas* book, the fabric was covered in little pictures of Santa Claus and Mrs. Claus and the sleigh with the reindeer. It was always our job to unwrap the book first and try to guess what the pajama material would look like. Sometimes the boys' pajamas were different material than the girls', but usually we all matched.

So it was that, from my very first Christmas until I was in my late teens, Aunt Anna made pajamas for me and every one of the grandkids. We'd wear those pajamas all year long–usually they were our only pajamas and somehow she always got the size just right. She picked material that was warm and soft and I felt loved every night when I put them on.

As I got older, there started to be years when I thought the pajama idea was for babies, and that I was much too grown up to wear matching pajamas with my siblings. I'd roll my eyes at the silly fabrics and moan with my sisters when we had to model the pajamas for the family on Christmas Eve. I'd seen the pretty nightgowns in department stores, and the nightshirts with cartoon characters and funny sayings that my friends had. That's what I wanted. I did not want to endure another year with home-made pajamas. Until the year that my Great-Aunt Anna got sick.

She'd come down with pneumonia from a dust storm that rolled over the desert that fall. Uncle Fred had tried to take care of her but he was really old, too. So my mom and my sisters and I left home and drove to New Mexico in October that year to take care of her. I got to stay home from school and help, but my mom made my sisters go to school down there. Aunt Anna was so sick she didn't get out of bed much and she couldn't play the piano. We made chicken soup the way she liked it with green chili and beans. We washed her beautiful gray hair and rolled it back into a loose bun, and we hung the laundry out on the line so the sun would kill the germs. Finally, she started to get better and by Christmas she was almost back to her old self. She could even play a song or two on the piano but she couldn't sing quite as loud as before. Everyone came for Christmas that year but there were no presents to open on Christmas Eve. Mom said we were getting too old for pajamas and Christmas books anyway. We were just so glad that Aunt Anna was feeling better that it didn't really matter.

That next fall was my first year of college. I was going to a big university, going to live in a dorm on campus, and be almost a hundred miles from home. I was nervous and excited and scared all at the same time. The day before I was to leave, a package arrived in the mail for me. It was from Aunt Anna. I smiled with my mom as I started opening the box, knowing that, yes, she was a little bit quirky but I loved her even more because of it. "I wonder what this could be...?" I said, jokingly. "Maybe she found some fabric with books and pencils all over it." We laughed together imagining the possibilities. Inside the box, the gift was wrapped in tissue so I lifted it out. It seemed a little bit big for pajamas. "Hmmm...?" For the split second before I opened it, I was perplexed. Then I got a glimpse and my heart skipped a beat.

Neatly folded inside the tissue was a quilt made of all the fabrics she had used over the years to make my pajamas. Together Mom and I carefully unfolded the quilt and draped it across the couch. We were speechless. It was a beautiful pattern, twelve different blocks, each its own unique star, but all together making one larger star in the middle. Then, around the outside edge, was a quilted border pattern called piano keys. Tears flooded my eyes as I ran my fingers over the fabric pieces, recalling the fun of pajamas made just for me, and the books that matched. Aunt Anna had saved the pieces and stitched each quilt block differently. Then finally, she framed the whole quilt in a light turquoise fabric. There was of course the cowboy material, and the dogs, the fishing material and I spotted the wild-flowers and the sheep. They were all there. Eighteen years of pajamas, but somehow when she put it all together, it was beautiful.

She could not have given me any gift more meaningful. Not only did I have the memories of each and every Christmas with my family and siblings, it reminded me of her. It was soft and beautiful, like she was, and wrapped around me twice just like her hugs.

ABOUT TRADITIONS

By Dorie Allington

Mom and I are in the kitchen talking, and I'm fixing our traditional ham for Christmas dinner. Before putting it in the pan, I slice off about two inches from each end. Mom looks at me and says, "What are you doing?"

"What you always did—cut off the end of the ham," I answer.

Mom bursts out laughing! When she at last catches her breath, she tells me: "When you were growing up, I didn't have a very big roasting pan. I had to do that so the ham would fit!"

A QUILTER'S PRAYER

by Dorie Allington

A needle, thread and stash of scraps,
good friends and heartfelt laughter,
Memories pieced and patched by hand
to hold in hearts thereafter...

Dear Lord, bless every stitch and seam
that bind these squares together,
For they are the patterns, pictures and hues
of people and times I treasure.

DECEMBER

10

And there were in the same country shepherds... keeping watch over their flock by night.

Luke 2:8

You probably wouldn't think about what it would be like to be a shepherd unless you actually had to raise sheep. We can learn a lot from taking care of animals, and sheep are no exception. In the Bible, people are compared to sheep quite a few times and it's not the most flattering comparison! They can be extremely stubborn animals, and a shepherd must be exceedingly patient and creative in his leading of the sheep.

A neighbor told a story about his lambs. He had many newborn lambs but one little lamb had been rejected by his mother. These little orphan lambs are called "bummer" lambs. When a lamb is rejected, the person caring for the sheep must step in and become like a mother to that baby lamb. That person, the shepherd, feeds and protects the lamb; that lamb becomes accustomed to his voice and learns to trust the shepherd completely.

We are all like little "bummer" lambs—in a good way. We all need tender loving care to survive. When we spend time with God, our Shepherd, we know His voice and we can follow Him to the safe places. He takes care of us and finds us when we get lost. Whenever danger is near, when we are injured or hungry, we know where to go. We go to the Shepherd.

Jesus the shepherd says, "Feed My Sheep." The "sheep" He is referring to are all His people. Gather food to give to a food pantry. Plan something your family can bake together to take to a person who is lonely. Nurture someone who is in a nursing home with a visit. Feed His sheep with gentle caring.

December 10

Little Miracles

by Cathy Atkinson

Susan and Jason had been honeymooning last Christmas, so this year they were especially looking forward to celebrating with each of their families. Susan's whole family would be at her parent's house; grandparents, aunts, uncles and cousins, some family she hadn't seen since the wedding. It would be a grand celebration, and with everyone bringing food, they'd be sure to have a feast. But Susan and Jason awoke Christmas Eve morning to a blizzard and two feet of snow already. It was not possible even to get their little car down the driveway.

Being the eternal optimist, Susan assumed that someone in a four-wheel-drive could make the trip out to their little country home to pick them up. Surely the snowplows were out clearing the roads in the city. But no. The deep snow had paralyzed the entire city. No one was going anywhere. It was heartbreaking to hear the merriment on the other end of the phone—at both houses their families were together, playing games and enjoying the day. Susan was jealous.

Here she was out in the middle of nowhere, with no presents to unwrap and not a single bit of holiday food (and none of her brothers and sisters to tease).

They hadn't been to the grocery store lately because money was tight and besides, there would be plenty of food at their family gatherings. Susan had been counting on the yummy Christmas dinner and leftovers to get them through the week. She took inventory of her kitchen cupboards. A box of macaroni and cheese and a loaf of banana bread. That was it. Macaroni and cheese for Christmas dinner? Uggghhhh! How could this be happening? This was the worst Christmas ever.

"Honey, I think you're going to want to see this." Jason interrupted her thoughts. He'd been outside shaking snow from the trees and shoveling the doorway entrances. Stomping his snowy boots on the backdoor rug he said, "Hurry, Sue, get your coat and hat and come with me." He sounded excited and she couldn't begin to fathom why. "Why? What?" She wasn't in the mood for games.

"Just come," he insisted. Susan begrudgingly pulled on her boots, grabbed her coat from the closet and donned a hat. An icy blast of wind hit them as they stepped into an all white world. OK, she had to admit, this was a bad storm. Jason grabbed her arm and they made their way to the garage. Once inside the garage, Jason walked quickly to the far corner where the boxes were piled.

"What is it, Jase?" Her fingers were icicles and the last thing she wanted to do was hang around in the garage. It was so incredibly cold.

He grabbed the edge of an old blue moving blanket laying on a shelf and pulled it aside. Susan couldn't believe what she saw. Curled up in the corner was their cat, Sunny, and four brand new kittens. Susan gasped, "Oh my gosh, they're so tiny! They don't even have their eyes open yet." She bent down and pick one up. "They're barely alive."

"I'm thinking they were born this morning sometime," Ben said. "It's a miracle they're alive. But they sure can't stay out here much longer or they'll freeze. We've got to get them inside."

Susan's frustration melted away as she gathered up two of the newborn kittens and tucked them inside her warm coat. These babies needed a warm safe place. She shuddered to think of what could have happened if she and Jason had been gone. The real reasons for Christmas suddenly came into focus—it wasn't about the presents and the food or the fun and games. Christmas meant caring for others, thanking God for His provisions, for His Son, and for all His blessings. This year that included four tiny miracles. Even with macaroni and cheese for dinner, Susan knew it would be a joy-filled Christmas Day.

NOT ONLY FOR CHRISTMAS

by John Greenleaf Whittier

Somehow, not only for Christmas,
But all the long year through,
The joy that you give to others
Is the joy that comes back to you.

And the more you spend in blessing
The poor and lonely and sad,
The more of your heart's possessing
Returns to make you glad.

December 11

For unto you is born
this day in the city of David a Saviour...
Christ the Lord.

Luke 2:11

Why was Bethlehem called the City of David? Because King David was on Joseph and Mary's family tree—he was a great-great-great-great (lots of greats)...grandfather. Even back in Bible times the legacy that family members left was important. Joseph and Mary knew very well who their ancestors were. It might seem easy to just forget about the lives of people in your family that have gone before you, and they might seem like strangers since you never really knew them. But your ancestors were real people with real jobs and families just like you. We can honor our family legacy by learning about our ancestors. Who knows, you might uncover some stories you hadn't known before!

Look at scrapbooks and family pictures together. Talk about the unique characteristics each family member has, and if another relative passed along that trait; for example, a quirky sense of humor, big feet, the way you laugh or walk. Then plan a time for making self-portrait cookies! Using cookie cutters and a traditional gingerbread or sugar cookie dough recipe, bake cookies representing each family member, and perhaps best friends and favorite relatives, too. Then keeping in mind of what makes each of you unique, create a self-portrait cookie that portrays your features, sense of style, and interests, such as wearing a favorite team jersey or putting a book, football, or pet in the arms.

DECEMBER 11

A FAMILY RESEMBLANCE

by Cathy Atkinson

"Sarah, look at this..." My husband's voice had a childlike excitement to it. "Oh, you're going to love this." He stood over and old box we had discovered tucked away in the back corner of the basement at his parent's house. He'd already opened the box, and had a pile of black and white pictures spread out on the table. Reaching into the box he pulled out a worn leather scrapbook and held it out for me.

"What is all this?" I asked, squealing with delight. "Who are these pictures of?"

"I think they are mostly my mom and dad growing up and my grandparents. Maybe some of my great-grandparents." He began sorting through the pictures while I sat down and opened the well-worn scrapbook. I didn't know these people, but you could definitely tell they were family.

Suddenly our girls, who had been playing in the next room, were standing on either side of me, wanting to see and asking questions. Suzanna, our youngest, was curious, like any three-year-old, but Lydia understood this was our family and she was full of questions.

"Who is that?" Lydia pointed at one picture.

"That's Grandma when she was a baby, and this one...is when she was about your age." I showed her a darling picture of John's mom at about five years old. She had a half-smile and beautiful dark curls cascading around her face and shoulders.

"Who is that?" Suzanna asked, turning to John, climbing into his arms. "What is that, Daddy?" Now she was on his knees, fingers into the photo piles, and trying to climb onto his shoulders. He looked at me with a grin, and looked back at her. "So much for sorting photos, huh, Suzi-Q." He lifted her high into the air and she laughed. "We didn't want to look at those old photos anyway, did we?"

Looking through this photo history gave me a sense of family. I loved the laughter and memories that had been captured here, the sense of family from the past and family continuing on. John had always jokingly commented when he saw family pictures that he had missed out on the look-alike genes that his brother and dad had shared. I had to admit, they did look a lot alike. But then again, I could see the family resemblance between John and his dad, too. It was just a little harder to pinpoint. It wasn't the nose or the hairline...I couldn't put my finger on it, but it was there.

Then I spotted a picture of John's grandmother as a little girl that looked so much like Lydia I was startled. "Oh my gosh," I said slowly... "Look, honey, you won't believe this." Holding the picture up for John to see, I waited for his response. He glanced up, casually. "Oh, wow," he said. "They do look a bit alike."

"A bit?" I teased him for understating the obvious. "A bit? They could be twins." I studied the photo again.

John paused and looked again. "Uh-huh. They have the same exact dark eyes. And the chin, I think...they have the same chin. And the hair, they have the same hair. Yeah, Ok, I'd say there is some family resemblance." We both looked at Lydia and smiled. I playfully turned her head to the side to get a better profile view.

"You, young lady, have a very strong family resemblance to your great-grandmother." She beamed with delight as if I'd just pronounced her Queen.

"Do I have a zemblnse, Mommy? Do I? Do I have one, too?" Suzanna's little upturned face was so hopeful, what could I say? Grabbing her up into my arms, I said, "Yes, Suzanna, you do, too!" I smothered her in kisses until she was giggling hysterically. "You look just like me! We have a family resemblance," I said, smiling at my young daughter.

Later that night, back at home and with the girls tucked in bed, John and I were watching TV when pajama clad Lydia padded barefoot into the room holding her Children's Bible. "Honey, what are you doing? You're supposed to be in bed asleep," I said, muting the TV.

"I know, but Mom, I was reading my Bible and I wanted to show you something," she said, walking over to me.

Setting the Bible on the arm of the sofa she continued, "There's a picture of Jesus in here somewhere." She flipped through the pages until she came upon a modern rendition of Jesus and the Children. "This one. Here. See this picture?"

"Um–hum, I see it."

"And, do you see?" Her little finger pointed to Jesus. She looked up at me. "Can you see it?"

"See what?" What was she talking about?

"Umm, the family resemblance?" I was doing everything I could not to giggle. Kids can say the funniest–and sweetest–things. "Why you're right, Lydia." I tried to sound surprised and impressed by her discovery. I glanced over at John who was grinning ear to ear, trying with all his might not to burst out laughing. Oh, this was a good one! Ha! John looks like Jesus? I knew he would milk this for all it was worth, but I had to keep a straight face for Lydia's sake.

She was totally serious, though, wasn't even cracking a smile. And she looked at me with such earnest childlike sincerity that it caught me off-guard. I looked back at the picture, and it suddenly dawned on me. She saw her Father. Lydia was seeing in Jesus' eyes the same unconditional love she'd seen in her own father eyes. That's what I saw between John and his dad. The family resemblance was in the love.

DECEMBER

12

Glory to God in the highest,
and on earth peace,
good will toward men....

Luke 2:14

Although nothing had taken place as Joseph and Mary would have planned, the very first Christmas happened exactly as God had intended it—perfectly imperfect. It was God's perfect plan and yet from a human viewpoint it seemed sort of messed up. No place to stay? Fine, a stable will work. No family around to help celebrate? No problem, we have shepherds and wise men, the innkeeper and a whole barn full of gentle animals to keep things moving along. No clothes for the baby? Here is some cloth perfect for swaddling. No welcoming party or baby shower? I'll send angels to sing and welcome Him. Regardless of the way things may have seemed at the time, it was indeed a glorious birth!

Many of us send cards and letters out at Chrismas time. It's always a highlight to receive a newsy letter from a dear friend, catching us up on their family happenings. And the pictures are wonderful, too. But in these busy days, it may be difficult for everyone to keep up with all the mail you receive. If someone has taken the time to send you a card, take the time to acknowledge them. Put all your cards in a basket on the table and each night, pull out one card to share with the whole family so all can stay connected with them. This is a tangible way we can keep long distance friends close to our hearts.

Have you sent out cards this year? It doesn't have to be anything elaborate—have your children draw a picture, make a few copies of it, jot a quick "thinking of you" and drop it in the mail. Your friends will love that you thought of them.

A SNOWY MORNING IN MARCH

by Cathy Atkinson

That morning, in the middle of the blizzard, we discovered two newborn baby goats huddled in the hay. According to my calculations they were two days early. Probably born an hour or so ago before we found them, they were weak and freezing cold. Neither of them could stand to drink the milk they so desperately needed. We quickly brought them inside, hoping to warm them near the woodstove. With warm towels, we dried them off, wrapped them up and tried to stimulate them to drink.

Finally, it seemed like they were both coming around, and were ready for some nourishment. It's hilarious tying to teach a baby goat to take to a store bought nipple. You end up with milk everywhere, and it's a sticky mess! We'd grabbed all our kitchen towels just trying to keep up with the milk squirting this way and that. My two sons and daughter and I were doubled over laughing at their funny antics as they worked to regain strength in their legs; little bounces and prances and attempts at jumping around the kitchen floor, usually ending in a heap of twisted legs.

We had erected a makeshift "fence" with the kitchen chairs, hoping to keep them contained, but it wasn't really working. At 10:00 a.m., it was feeding time again, and so we took turns holding the makeshift bottles while and slurped that yummy milk.

It was still snowing hard outside so we were surprised to hear a knock at the front door. Who could that be? My oldest son hopped the "fence" and opened the door with me right behind him. There on my front porch all bundled up like a mama penguin and her babies, were three smiling faces I did not recognize.

I opened the screen door, and the tall mama penguin in the red coat said in a somewhat muffled voice, "Hi, we live around the corner and we were out for a walk this morning and we decided to come introduce ourselves."

My stomach did a double flip. I motioned for them to come inside, and suddenly I was incredibly self-conscious about the house. Dirty kitchen towels and bottles of goat milk were everywhere, there was a goat in the kitchen, and I was standing in the living room with a goat in my arms! This was not the impression I'd wanted to make, but I took a deep breath and decided I'd try to make the best of it. I handed the little goat to my daughter, smiled and asked if we could take their coats and would she like a cup of tea?

As her son and daughter scampered off to play with my kids, I noticed she had a beautiful smile and kind, loving eyes. She stuck out her hand and said, "My name's Robin." Her voice was muffled, or... like she was under water. I could understand her, but it was like listening to someone with an accent.

Stepping over our make-shift fence, I motioned for her to sit down as I turned to the stove to put the tea kettle on. I said, "I'm so glad you came over but you must be wondering..."

She interrupted me mid-stream. "I'm deaf," she said. "I read lips so you need to be facing me when we talk."

I turned back around. "You're deaf?" I was amazed. "How...how do you do it? Don't you use sign language?"

"No, I learned to read lips when I was young and I never learned sign language—at least not much."

"You can read my lips and you can speak, but you can't hear me?" I must have sounded like a first grader, still processing what this meant.

"Yep," she smiled. "And I love your baby goats!" Suddenly I realized how silly I had been–the messy house, the farm animals in the messy house, none of that was as important as Robin herself. I had been afraid she'd think my life a bit too crazy for her. But I took a chance on friendship and I'm so glad I did. I gained a lifetime friend when I invited Robin in to have a cup of tea with me—and the goats—that snowy morning in March.

December 13

The shepherds said one to another,
Let us now go even unto Bethlehem,
and see this thing which is come to pass,
which the Lord hath made known unto us.
And they came with haste, and found Mary,
and Joseph, and the babe lying in a manger.
And when they had seen it, they made known
abroad the saying which was told them
concerning this child.

Luke 2:15–17

Everyone who heard about Jesus' birth was amazed. Amazed and excited about God's good news, just as the shepherds were. Our good news is the same today as it was that night when the angels sang: God has given us the gift of His Son. With the coming of Christmas, we welcome the blessings of our faith. Each year as we look forward to hearing the age old stories, our faith grows deeper. It becomes a part of who we are, reflected in all we do and say.

We see faith all around us this season. It is expressed in many of our traditional carols. We read about it in stories, watch it happening in a movie. Seeing faith in others stirs something in our own hearts—a connection, a love. We walk into church on Christmas Eve and sense the holiness of this night. We sing *Silent Night* or *Oh Come All Ye Faithful* and get tears in our eyes and a lump in our throats. That feeling is your heart connecting with God—because of your faith. Even the faith we have is a gift from God, and it grows stronger and deeper at Christmas.

Everyone loves to hear carolers as they sing around the neighborhood. It's a great way to spend an evening of laughter and fun. Gather together a group of friends and decide ahead of time the songs you enjoy and want to sing. If you have musically inclined friends who harmonize, that is great. If not, it absolutely doesn't matter because it's not all about the singing. Caroling is all about bringing the joy of Christmas to others.

If it's not possible to carol from house to house in your neighborhood, go to a nursing home or senior center. The happy Christmas music may warm even a Scrooge's heart. This is an easy activity to pull off, requires very little advance preparation or purchases, and will guarantee to put a smile on all within earshot.

A Lesson Learned

by Laurie Harper

It was time once again for the traditional Christmas progressive dinner. Being only 8 years old, I thought the idea of eating just a portion of a meal at different houses made no sense at all, but I did enjoy playing with all my cousins as there were a lot of us, ranging in age from newborn to age 20. Each house also provided a complete diversity of toys and games, so as much as I hated to admit it, I did look forward to the progressive dinner about as much as my parents.

We started the evening at our house. Mom had crackers and cheese, and my absolute favorite, cocktail weenies in barbeque sauce. My favorite cousin, Megan, who was two years younger than me, and I had just started another game of cards, when we were told it was time to go to Grandma's house for homemade chicken and noodles and rolls. I closed my eyes and could already smell those homemade rolls!

From Grandma's house, we would make our way to Aunt Teri's and Uncle Doug's. Megan and I could hardly wait to get the signal to go to their house because Aunt Teri and Uncle Doug lived in a huge, old farmhouse. The very best part about their house was our older cousin's upstairs bedroom. Her room was like a dream room for me and Megan. We planned our strategy of how we would abandon the other cousins so we could have this glorious bedroom all to ourselves.

As we played Christmas music and did our hair, it was Megan who noticed how quiet the house seemed. We both ran downstairs only to discover we were home alone! Suddenly this huge farmhouse that we loved had creaky floors and scary shadows and sounds from outside that stopped Megan and me in our tracks. I looked at Megan and told her I didn't even know what house everyone was at. She smiled and said she knew because her mom was making the desserts.

As I stood there afraid to even move, I watched my younger cousin go into action. She calmly turned on some house lights, found the phone and dialed her house. I was still in shock that they all left without us!

Megan said her mom told her that she and her dad had left the farm early to get the desserts ready and apparently everyone thought we had left with them. Since we were tucked away in the upstairs bedroom playing Christmas music, we did not hear the signal that it was time to go to the next house. Well, surely they were worried and riddled with guilt. Were they all coming back to the farmhouse to get us? Were we to call the police?

Megan said they were making our oldest cousin drive the 10 miles back to get us. I asked her if she thought they were filled with guilt and shame—embarrassed that they forgot two precious young girls. Megan nodded her head "no" and had the same look of disbelief as me.

When our cousin and uncle finally arrived for us, they had no sympathy at all for Megan and me and seemed more interested in getting back to the desserts than us. It wasn't much better when we got to Megan's house. There were only a few Christmas cookies left and a pitiful "sorry" from the entire group.

Once again I was surprised as my younger cousin just seemed to take everything in stride, and I heard her telling her rendition of our experience to a group of cousins. She made it sound as if it was really nothing at all and actually kind of fun being left behind in that spooky farmhouse with all the lights off and sounds of coyotes and owls outside.

It occurred to me that I had one smart cousin as she retold the experience to our younger cousins and I saw the look of admiration and awe on their faces as they listened to her.

I learned a valuable lesson that night from my little cousin, Megan. I realized that even when things don't go as planned, your attitude on any given situation is what makes a difference. You can take pity on yourself and blame others, or you can take charge and handle it in a positive way.

We will always be known in our family as the "forgotten girls" but it was the life lesson I learned that night from my little cousin that will never be forgotten.

DECEMBER 14

*Where is he that is born
King of the Jews? for we have seen
his star in the east,
and are come to worship him.*

Matthew 2:2

Jesus, the Light of the World, is the reason behind all the lights at Christmas. He is the Light of the World. His Light helps us understand God's plan and shows us which way to go, which decisions to make.

The beauty of the lights at Christmas is in the variety and colors. The differences make them even more beautiful. As God's children, we shine like the sparkling lights of Christmas, each of us unique and a little bit different than the other. Every one of us has a different job to do, illuminating a specific part of the bigger picture. My little light shines on what God wants for me and your light is perfect for you. So, don't hide your light—let it shine for all to see!

Celebrate together by enjoying the beautiful lights of the season. Put on some music and work together to put the Christmas lights up at your house. Pile in the car, sing along to a radio station playing Christmas music, and drive around town at night to see all the pretty Christmas decorations. If your town has a Parade of Lights, put it on your calendar and get your hot chocolate ready to go!

Take a Glow–Walk at night. First, have a flashlight and paper lunch bag for each person. Draw and cut out holes, such as a star shape, from the bag. Secure the opened bag just over the top of the flashlight and hold it there with a rubber band. Now turn on your flashlights and illuminate your night walk!

THE LITTLE CANDLE

By Doris Carter Wardlow

A story is told about a mountain village and a Christmas of years past.

On a cold winter night a special service was to be held at the little church in the village. One family prepared for the long walk to the church, almost a mile away.

Everyone was dressed in their warmest and best except for little Danny, too sick with a cold, and his grandma who would look after him. There was a good deal of rummaging and chatter as those who were going gathered up lanterns and all the candles they could, which would be lit at the end of the service, and most of the candles were put into pockets for the trip. "This one's no good," one child said, tossing a small candle aside, "too small, and broken besides." "Leave it here—it's worthless. Let's get going." And they set off.

Grandma sat by the little boy's bed and rocked, humming carols to him. Then she heard the wind against the window pane. This was going to be a very bad storm—and her family was out in it.

Not sure how much time had passed, she peered out the window looking for her loved ones, worried they were lost in the dark as the winds were still blowing too hard to keep their candles lit.

From his bed, Danny said, "Light the tiny candle, Grandma, and set it in the window. Maybe it can guide them home." So that's what the grandmother did. She pulled her wrap closer around her shoulders, stood by the window, waiting, watching, and praying.

At long last, she saw figures emerging from the woods. "Thank you, Lord," she whispered. They pushed away the snow and made their way into the warm house, snow sticking to their hats and faces and shoulders. The poor family was nearly frozen.

"We were going in circles in the woods—until we saw the tiny flicker in the dark—and we followed its light." The fire was stoked, quilts brought out to wrap around them, and cups of hot tea warmed their hands as they gathered to tell their story. The light that had been rejected was still the one that saved them and guided them home.

DECEMBER 14

THE LEGEND OF THE LIGHTHOUSE

By Doris Carter Wardlow

Along a rugged craggy coast
a stately lighthouse stood,
sending forth its shining beams,
helping seafarers all it could.

This one wintry Christmas night,
or so the legend's told,
one hardened veteran mariner
had wandered from the fold.

His seaman's knowledge had failed him
and he didn't sense the storm.
His old eyes never saw the signs
as the blizzard clouds took form.

The blackened water caught him up
and tossed him to and fro.
How he would ever reach the shore
he surely didn't know.

At one time he'd felt close to God
but through years, he'd drifted away.
Now faith rose in his heart once more
as the old man began to pray...

December 14

"Dear Lord, I ask your guidance
for I'm lost upon the sea.
I put this vessel into your hands
and I place my trust in thee..."

No sooner had he said these words
a voice said "Steer to right".
Was his old mind playing tricks?
he asked, but he turned with all his might.

A flash of light revealed the giant
boulder that grazed his boat.
He didn't question further–
The voice had kept his craft afloat.

In the foggy distance, now he saw
the sign he'd waited for:
The lighthouse with its steady beam
guiding him back to shore.

"It's you, Lord, isn't it?", asked the man,
his heart longing to be sure.
"I am with you," came the answer,
then these words, clear and pure:

*"I am the Arms that carried you through
the darkest times you've known–
I am the Voice you hear in the night
And the Light that leads you home."*

DECEMBER

15

...and, lo, the star,
which they saw in the east,
went before them, till it came and stood
over where the young child was.
When they saw the star,
they rejoiced with exceeding great joy.

Matthew 2:9–10

They didn't call them Wise Men for nothing. They really were wise. They were scientists; scholars who had studied both the stars and the scriptures. They knew what this sign in the sky meant, and it was so important to them that they packed up their belongings, and headed out. It probably took them two years to get to where Jesus was.

That's a long time to follow something unless you are very convinced it is true. It isn't hard to imagine why they were so overjoyed when the star finally stopped and stood still—right over the house where Jesus lived. Sometimes we can feel very small, looking up at the millions of stars in the sky. Isn't it amazing to think that 2000 years ago Wise Men looked at the same night sky that we see? And just as the Wise Men "rejoiced" when they saw the star, we feel the same sense of joy.

On a beautiful clear night spread a blanket on the ground outside and look up at the sky full of stars. Maybe you have a telescope, or have access to one. Take some time to study the stars, the Milky Way, and the moon. Can you identify any of the constellations? Even those who are not very familiar with astronomy can usually spot The Big Dipper. Think about how it must have been for those Wise Men, scientists who actually studied the stars, to see a brand new star in the sky. Isn't it amazing that in this vast universe, God sees every part of your life, each singular event and every need? He can send a miracle just when needed. He cares for you that much.

ANGELS IN BLUE JEANS

by Sue Englert

The door to their room opened, and their mom burst in shouting, "Wake up! The house is on fire!" Jennie, the younger sister, gasped as she sat up, taking in a huge breath of smoke-filled air, which made her cough uncontrollably. Samantha, the older sister, jumped from her bed, put her arms around Jennie, and gently but quickly guided her out of the room.

The whole family, all five children and Mom and Dad, gathered in the second floor hallway. They knew they had to act soon in order to get out alive. Dad said, "Come on! This way," and everyone followed him back into Samantha and Jennie's bed-room where he was trying to open a window. The window was stuck and wouldn't budge—while the smoke continued to get thicker and thicker, making it harder and harder to breathe. "Stand back," Dad said as he picked up the desk chair and bashed it through the window, sending shards of glass flying everywhere. Then, using his bare hands, he cleared the remaining jagged-edged pieces of glass from the window frame. He quickly started lifting his children out onto the small roof above the back door into the cold Christmas night.

Samantha looked around at the snow on the ground and the icicles on the trees, and she wondered how they would get down and what they would do next. Once everyone was on the rooftop, Dad lowered Daniel, the oldest brother, toward the ground, holding tight to his hands in two secure handshakes between father and son. Daniel ran to the garage and came back with a ladder. As Samantha was preparing to climb down the ladder, Jennie tugged on Mom's nightgown and shouted, "Look! In the driveway!"

There stood two young men in blue jeans and winter coats, strangers, standing and staring in shock at the family gathered on the small rooftop.

"Come and help us!" Mom shouted. The two young men opened the gate and came into the yard. As soon as her toes reached the snowy patio, one of the young men handed Samantha their two winter coats, still warm from their bodies.

"We were driving down the street and we saw smoke coming from the windows," one of them said, "Please, take our coats so you can keep warm." They wrapped Samantha and Jennie in one coat and the two youngest brothers, Christopher and George, in the other coat. Mom ran across the street to see if she could wake the neighbors while the two young men helped everyone else into the garage for the little bit of shelter it would provide.

As the fire trucks pulled up, Mom and their neighbor, Mr. Monroe, came to get everyone from the garage and take them across the street, where Mrs. Monroe was making hot chocolate and coffee. Snuggled under a quilt on the big soft sofa, Mom cried and wondered aloud what they would do now. "Here it is, Christmas night, and our house is burning—everything we have is going up in smoke," she sobbed, "And the Christmas presents! Oh, all of your Christmas presents will be gone!"

Mrs. Monroe came in from the kitchen with a tray of steaming mugs of hot chocolate and coffee, set it down on the coffee table, and said, "Right now, let's not worry about that. Everyone got out safe, and you are all here, warm and alive." She looked at the two youngest boys, still cocooned in the big winter coat, and asked, "Whose coat is that?" Samantha and Jennie had just wriggled out of the other coat.

Mom said, "Two young men stopped to help and gave us their coats." When Dad and Mr. Monroe finally came inside, as the firemen were working on the last flames of the smoldering house, Mom asked him about the two young men. He said they were gone, and he hadn't thought to ask for their names or phone numbers. In fact, no one could remember exactly what the young men looked like or how old they seemed to be. Finally, from inside the cozy cocoon of the big winter coat, the youngest brother, George, smiled and proudly announced, "I guess they were our Christmas angels!" Everyone else laughed and nodded in agreement. Even though there would be many challenges ahead, they had been the blessed recipients of a real Christmas miracle after all.

DECEMBER

16

And when they had opened their treasures, they presented unto him gifts; gold, and frankincense and myrrh.

Matthew 2:11

Have you ever had the experience of giving the perfect gift? The giver of the gift gets as much (or even more) pleasure in the giving than the re-cipient does in getting. God's gifts are showered on us everyday. He enjoys the pleasure of giving and He is creative in the gifts He gives. He personalizes each gift, knowing exactly what it takes to make us jump up and down with delight: A sunset, a new baby, a healing touch, the smile of a friend. That little baby in the manger was the ultimate gift. It cost Him everything and was perfect for each one of us. God loves us and thinks we're worth it. We enjoy gift-giving because it is fun to let the other person know we love them and think they're worth it, too.

Experience the joy of giving without expecting anything in return. Instead of overloading on gifts for each other, your family might decide to give to a charity that has a special meaning for the family. Or, give to several charities based on each family member's interests. For example, if you have young children, you might plan an afternoon to shop with your family for small gifts to fill a Christmas shoe box (or boxes) that can be sent to children in need around the world.

Perhaps one child has a love for animals and would like to donate to a rescue, another might want to give to a campaign supporting a cure for an illness a friend deals with. Instead of the focus being on what you might get, this turns the spotlight around to what you can give.

CRAFTED WITH LOVE

By Cathy Atkinson

When my mom, Sharon, was six years old she got a pair of skis for Christmas. My grandfather had fashioned them himself from the trunk of the old Silver Maple after it was hit by lightening that summer. All summer and fall he had worked in the shed, keeping the secret gift hidden under a heavy brown tarp in the rafters when he wasn't there. Cut precisely and sanded slippery smooth, he stained them a rich golden hue that almost glowed golden in the winter sun. Stroke after stroke he had rubbed sticky wax along the grain until it brought out a soft velvety gloss and healed fast what had previously been coarse and unfinished.

He knew the maple would be strong and durable. The front ends turned up evenly and then gracefully narrowed to perfect points. Leather straps, nailed to the middle of each piece, were long enough to wrap around and secure her boots tightly. On the narrow inside edge of one ski he carefully carved "To Sharon." On the other ski, "With Love from Dad, 1939." Standing back, he smiled. He could hardly wait to give them to her.

From the time she could walk, Sharon had been on skis. She'd learned to ski by standing on the tops of her dad's boots, arms tucked around behind his legs. Every Saturday morning all winter long they would drive up to the little ski area on the mountain. She loved to ski, but the best part was being together.

That Christmas morning Sharon got up early. She wasn't really expecting a gift since money was tight and they had talked about how simple their Christmas would be. So, settling into a warm spot on the floor next to the wood stove, she gazed lovingly at the pretty tree. It was so beautiful with the colorful string of electric lights that reflected off the silvery icicles and glass ornaments. And then she noticed—and giggled to herself—there were, in fact, bulges in the stockings that hung under the big window.

Finally, Mom and Dad were ready and with Merry Christmas hugs they handed out their stockings. There was an orange and two large pieces of red and green striped ribbon candy in each stocking. No one said anything about the tall wooden skis that sat silently tucked behind the tree.

They all ate a breakfast of oatmeal with thick cream and maple syrup drizzled over the top. After breakfast they played dominoes and read the

Christmas story from the family Bible. Finally my grandfather, with a twinkle in his eye, said, "Sharon, why don't you go look behind the tree."

"What?" she asked, standing up and walking towards the tree. "Over here?" He nodded. Curious, she pulled aside the lower branches and caught a glimpse of a red ribbon. Her heart skipped a beat. Now her dad was standing next to her, lifting the precious gift from its hiding place.

"These are for you, Little-Pea," he said. His voice was rough with emotion but she didn't notice. A little gasp of joy escaped from her lips. She couldn't take her eyes off the beautiful skis.

He saw a look in her eyes and knew he had hit the mark—she truly loved this gift. She was too young to be able to comprehend what it had taken to make them—the hours of labor, the sacrifice of time. That didn't matter. Suddenly she was jumping with excitement. "Can we go skiing today, Daddy?"

He laughed, "Well, I suppose that's what they're for. Get yourself dressed. I'll take you out."

She snuggled close in his arms as he bent low next to her. "Thank you, Daddy," she said. "It's the very best Christmas present I've ever gotten."

"You're very welcome, Little–Pea." Smiling, he kissed her light brown curls, then held her away from himself to get a good look. Her absolute joy and excitement bubbled over, filling him with delight as well. He hadn't felt this happy in a very long time and he knew she was right. It was the very best Christmas gift he'd ever gotten.

With a grin and a tease in his voice, he said, "Well, hurry and get ready, Sharon! Let's go skiing!"

December 17

God so loved the world,
that he gave his only begotten Son...

John 3:16

As children, often times it doesn't occur to us that Christmas is celebrated in different ways around the world. We think everyone celebrates the way we do. That usually changes in about second grade. That's about the time we learn about "Christmas Around the World." Our eyes are suddenly opened to all kinds of new games and new foods and different types of celebrations. But always at the center of it all, the story of Jesus, born in a manger to Mary and Joseph. The types of observances around the world are as varied as the types of people. But the common thread across cultures and continents is Jesus himself. It's fun to realize that we are a part of God's family all around the world.

Choose a tradition from a different culture and try your hand at making, creating or experiencing it. You might have friends or neighbors who celebrate with special stories or recipes and would be delighted to help you. For example, make a Christmas piñata, fill it with candy and invite the neighbor children over for a piñata breaking party. You might learn to bake Greek Baklava, English Figgie Pudding, or Danish Butter Cookies. Try a new game, sing a new song. What is interesting and different about Christmas in the culture you chose, and what is the same as yours?

THE LEGEND OF THE POINSETTIA

as adapted by Patricia Mitchell

It was the custom in a tiny village in Mexico that all the children should bring a gift to the Baby Jesus at Christmas time. But one little girl was so poor that she had nothing to offer Him. On Christmas Eve, the girl looked up and gazed at all the stars twinkling above her. "I wish I could give the Baby Jesus all the stars in the sky!" she sighed, but she was very sad for she had nothing at all—much less a star—to bring him.

As church bells rang, she walked empty handed to the tiny village church. She was still thinking about the stars. Then her eyes fell on some wild-flowers growing at the side of the road. She stopped and quickly gathered a handful of the humble flowers. She heard someone say, "Those are only weeds!" A hot tear rolled off her cheek and onto the blossoms.

The little girl entered the candle-lit church, and she joined all the other children around the Baby Jesus. He was surrounded by gifts: Christmas candy, sugar cookies, sweet oranges, little wooden toys. When it came the girl's turn, she gently laid her flowers near His head. "Merry Christmas, Baby Jesus," she whispered as she knelt by the manger–bed and closed her eyes in prayer. When she opened her eyes, she put her hand to her mouth in wonder. In place of the wildflowers she had given the Baby Jesus was an array of majestic red star–shaped blooms! Her humble gift of love became the most beautiful gift of all. And from that time on, the poinsettia has been known as the Flower of the Holy Night.

Blessed is the season which engages the whole world in a conspiracy of love.

Hamilton Wright Mabie

EVERYWHERE, EVERYWHERE CHRISTMAS TONIGHT

by Phillips Brooks

Everywhere, everywhere, Christmas tonight!
Christmas in lands of the fir–tree and pine,
Christmas in lands of the palm–tree and vine,
Christmas where snow peaks stand solemn and white,
Christmas where cornfields stand sunny and bright...
Christmas where peace, like a dove in its flight
Broods o'er brave men in the thick of the fight;
For the Christ–child who comes is the Master of all,
No palace too great and no cottage too small;
The angels who welcome Him sing from the height...
Everywhere, everywhere, Christmas tonight.

December 18

For we are...
created in Christ Jesus
unto good works...

Ephesians 2:10

God created people, but He also created all the delightful animals. From the very beginning of time animals have been part of His plan. Isn't it wonderful that God, who could have chosen any place in the world to be born, chose a place surrounded by animals? God uses animals in our lives to protect us, feed us, clothe us, assist us, entertain us, to be companions for us, and the list goes on and on.

DECEMBER 18

We have a job to care for His creatures and creation. We may or may not be animal lovers, but we do have a responsibility to be respectful and kind to God's creatures. It can be easy to ignore the impact animals have in our lives, but taking care of an animal is a good chance for us to give this holiday season. Don't overlook your animal friends this Christmas!

Decorate an outside tree with ornaments that the birds will enjoy. Choose an evergreen tree if possible so that there will be additional shelter within its branches for the birds to enjoy the feast. Be sure to choose a tree that you can see from a window so your family will be able to watch the birds and you will see when the food needs replacing.

There are many different options of Christmas treats for your birds. One idea is to gather pinecones, cover with peanut butter and then roll in a bowl of birdseed. Hang from the tree with short loops of natural twine. Another idea is to use a needle and thread to string popcorn, and cranberries, peanuts, apple and orange slices. Taking care of God's creatures is one of our responsibilities as His children, and something fun your family can enjoy together.

DECEMBER 18

THE ATTIC'S SECRET

By Doris Carter Wardlow

"What was that?," the farmwife asked her husband. They were settled before the fireplace in their 125-year-old farm house. She was writing lists of things she wanted to accomplish before Christmas. He was reading his Scriptures.

"There it is again." Hesitation. They eyed one another, revealing to each other their curiosity...and wariness. "Sounds like it's coming from the attic."

Now they didn't believe in ghosts. And they were accustomed to the sounds of their old house as it settled. The cold was finally coming on after a mild autumn and the house was a gentle giant, squeaking, creaking and groaning as if snuggling in a little deeper for a winter's nap.

This was a strange sound, not one the friendly old two-story house had ever voiced before. They listened. They wondered.

The next evening, just as they were settling in at dusk, the noises started again. "Must be a varmint," the farmer said. But that was not very reassuring. What kind of varmint? A bird desperately trying to get out of the house? A snake? A rat? None of these possible options led to a comfortable feeling, nor a restful sleep.

The man would explore the high attic rafters, walls, and floorboards and the sounds would grow silent. Each day, they would start up again. It seemed as though something was eating up the house. As the temperatures dropped, the sounds only increased and grew more frantic.

Then one day, the farmer spied the culprit. High up on the side of the house, a flash of brown fur, a bushy tail, a small squirrel darted into a louvered vent. My, what a racket that little rascal could make! The man chuckled that this critter could consume so much of their worries. She sure had their imaginations going! But the fact remained, it was a nuisance, a very menacing noise in their comfortable life, and the damage that could be done to their structure was of great concern. Drastic measures would have to be taken.

Just then the squirrel reappeared from the attic vent with a mouthful of...cotton candy?! Were his eyes playing tricks on him?, the farmer wondered. The squirrel then made a bold leap onto a limb one would never have imagined she could have reached, and with lightning speed and amazing balance she scurried high up to a large knot hole of the giant walnut tree. The man peered up and there he saw the evidence of all the work the little squirrel had done over the weeks. The knot hole was completely lined, not with cotton candy, but with the pink insulation stolen from the attic. The squirrel had her little house all ready for winter.

The farmer couldn't help but admire the squirrel's resourceful and ingenious plan. And he sure appreciated a hard worker. "Ah well," the farmer thought, resigning himself to the fact that no drastic measures would be taken. "It's nearly Christmas."

In spring, four tiny squirrel babies came into the world on pink blankets, high up in a walnut tree.

December 19

*Fix these words of mine in
your hearts and minds...
Teach them to your children,
talking about them when you sit
at home and when you walk along the road,
when you lie down and when you get up.*

Deuteronomy 11:18–19 NIV

There are hundreds of wonderful, heartwarming Christmas story books that really bring home the meaning and message of Christmas. Your family must have favorites. Many stories are beautifully illustrated, magical in the plot, imaginative and just plain fun. One thing parents can do as our kids grow up is help them to differentiate between reality and fantasy. What seems ridiculously obvious to us, may not be to a young child.

There is absolutely nothing wrong with enjoying a good Christmas tale. But Jesus' birth should not be lumped in with all the other Christmas stories. The birth of Christ is recorded in the Bible which puts it in a class all by itself. It is The Story. As you enjoy all the delightful childrens' books this season, be sure to make a distinction between what we believe is true, what is fiction, and what is Divine!

Play a story-telling and word-building game. In turn, each person tells a sentence or more of an original story with the next person picking up where the last person left off. The most fun place to leave off is in the middle of a sentence ("and in the snow, he found a ...") leaving an opportunity for a big switch in theme. Surprising additions to the cast of characters will also give your story a chance to take an unexpected turn. Your story may be heartwarming, funny, or mysterious. Who knows?

THE LEGEND OF THE SNOW ANGEL

by Doris Carter Wardlow

On a faraway mountainside a long time ago, a little shepherd boy was guarding his sheep. The snow had been falling all day, and though he had spent many nights in the mountains by himself, on this particular night he felt afraid. Perhaps because of the heavy snow...or the growing darkness of the starless sky...this night was different.

The boy tried to find shelter, but there was none. Then he watched the ewes, walking around and back and forth, moving the snow with the push of their noses to make a little bed for themselves.

So the boy lay down in the snow, closed his eyes, and moved his arms and legs back and forth to smooth out a place to sleep. When he stood up to survey his work, he saw that in the snow there was the perfect form of a beautiful angel! This warmed his heart and his fear began to fade. He bundled into his blankets and in the night he fell asleep.

As morning light came and the bright sun kissed his face, he arose to an astonishing sight. There was a circle around him in the snow, for it appeared angel wings had brushed the snow around him! It was then that the boy realized he had been guarded by a circle of angels all the dark night long.

So the legend began those many years ago that hovering angels had stood guard over a little shep-herd boy who made the first Snow Angel. And it's still true to this day...

If you make a Snow Angel–
Angels in heaven will see
And will hover over you
And surround you
And give you Peace.

DECEMBER

20

I bring you good tidings of great joy, which shall be to all people.

Luke 2:10

Jesus' birthday is almost here! Are you ready to celebrate? Are the decorations in place and the presents wrapped? Have you done all you wanted to prepare for this special day?

Getting our hearts ready for the Celebration is the whole purpose of Advent. Every day this month you have opened a door on the Advent calendar, read a Bible verse and talked about what Christmas means. Every week you light a candle on the Advent wreath. Through the weeks, the excitement grows in anticipation of the birthday of Jesus. Christmas is the most wonderful time of the year!

What is the best gift you have ever received for Christmas? What's the best gift you've ever given? If you could give a birthday gift to Jesus, what would it be?

Everybody loves a birthday party! Plan a birthday party for Jesus. Make a birthday cake, with each person taking part in the preparation and decorating. Oh...and eating! Put 2 candles on Jesus' cake, one for each 1,000 years.

Give Jesus the best birthday gift of all—do something kind for someone. Pass out pieces of paper to every family member. Have each person write or draw a picture of something they can give Jesus. Perhaps Dad wants to help his elderly parents around the home. Maybe brother wants to promise Jesus he will stop teasing his sister so much. Or sister wants to remember to walk the dog more often. Perhaps Mom would like to give Jesus a gift by being more patient during homework time. Put the slips of paper in a small box and wrap it up with pretty paper. Put a tag on it which reads: TO JESUS and place it under your tree or by your nativity scene.

THE STORY OF THE FIRST CHRISTMAS GIFT

by Patricia Mitchell

On that first Christmas night, a poor shepherd boy on a faraway pasture heard astonishing news. "A King has been born! A King has been born..." echoed across the fields. "In a manger in Bethlehem..." came the message. "In Bethlehem!"rang through the hills.

As the shepherd boy pondered these words, his heart overflowed with joy. "I must go see this King!" he said to the shepherds who were with him, but the other shepherds just laughed. "A King!" they hooted. "So you're going to go visit a King? And what, pray tell, do you plan to bring him?" And they laughed even harder.

"It's true," the shepherd boy murmured as he started toward Bethlehem in search of the manger. "I can't go visit a King without bringing a valuable gift." As he traveled the dark path, he spotted a bright white pebble gleaming in the moonlight. He bent down to pick it up, and it was smooth to his hand and lovely to look at. The shepherd boy put the pebble in his pocket, because he planned to keep it. Now this pebble was his one and only possession.

When he arrived at the manger and saw the Baby, his joy turned to heartwarming love. He reached into his pocket. "I want You to have this," he whispered as he slipped the stone into the Baby's little hand. "When You see it, please remember how much I love You."

Of all the rich gifts the Holy Child received from that day forward, He always treasured His first gift, the little stone. To the King of Kings, it stood for the most valuable gift of all—a gift from the heart.

What can I give Him,
Poor as I am?
If I were a shepherd
I would bring a lamb.
If I were a Wise Man
I would do my part—
Yet what I can, I give Him:
Give my heart.

Christina Rossetti

DECEMBER

21

It is more blessed to give than to receive.

Acts 20:35

One of the best parts about life is that we have the chance to give to others. It's a learned character trait, modeled by those we love and trust. Babies and toddlers are not likely to give generously. What's in their hand is theirs, they want to keep it, and sharing does not usually come naturally. Those little people have no idea that life does not revolve around them. As we get older, however, we see the needs in others' lives and want to help. If we have experienced compassion from others, we learn how to show it. If we have grown up in an environment of acceptance and love, we will be people who are loving. The amazing thing is that the more we give to others, that is when we are happiest, and the more we receive in return. Who do you know in your life that is an especially giving person? What can you give of yourself this Christmas?

Draw names within your family to be Secret Elves for this next week. Shhh! Don't tell anyone whose name you drew! Think of three kind things you can do for your family member during the week. Maybe it's a small thing such as putting a chocolate on his or her pillow before bed at night. Perhaps you could get up early and do a chore that they don't like doing. How about bringing them breakfast in bed with the newspaper on a weekend morning? Or, offer to help babysit so he or she can get some last minute shopping done. On Christmas morning, take turns guessing the identity of each person's Secret Elf.

MY CHRISTMAS ANGEL

by Cathy Atkinson

My sophomore year of high school I played on the varsity soccer team, hoping someday to play in college. That dream was dashed when I came down on my knee at a crazy angle, tearing tendons and ligaments. Surgery was scheduled for the morning of December 22, just three days before Christmas.

After surgery, when I was settled into a room, the pain started to kick in. I was prepared for pain, but when I asked for some medication, the nurse gave me an over-the-counter pain reliever. She explained that since I was scheduled to go home the next day, the new protocol was to cut way back on the strong pain meds and try to get by on as little as possible. I figured I could handle it, and heading home sooner sounded like a good plan.

I could not, however, have been more wrong. Over the next couple hours I plunged to such a depth of pain that I couldn't really function. Heading home was the last thing on my mind. I couldn't eat, sleep, talk. It was not possible for me to focus on anything except the next immediate moment. My parents became concerned and talked to the nurses.

December 21

They decided I needed stronger medicines for the pain, but it would take a while to kick in. All that night I laid awake, tossing and turning, trying my hardest to be brave.

I had pushed my nurse's call button twice but no one came. It was the middle of the night and quiet in the hallway. My whole body hurt. I felt so alone and close to the end of my ability to hold myself together. Finally a nurse or aid walked in. I hadn't seen her before but it didn't matter. I figured she was covering for my regular nurse. I asked if I could please have some more pain medicine. She looked at my chart and said sympathetically, "No, I'm afraid not. I'm so sorry." She gently explained that it hadn't been long enough since the last dose. I was in so much pain that I couldn't stop my tears.

She filled my pitcher with fresh ice water and poured me a glass. Then she held it up to my lips so I could sip. She asked if I wanted her to stay and talk for awhile. Thinking I might feel less panicky if someone was there, I said yes, and she sat down. We talked about pets and I told her we had a black lab named Cody. Cody was my best friend and confidant. The nurse showed me a pin she had attached to her jacket–it was a black lab. Listening to her soft voice and feeling an occasional pat on the hand soothed and relaxed me until I fell right asleep.

The first thing I remembered when I woke up was how wonderful that nurse was. I wanted to thank her. So, when the morning nurse came in, I asked him about the nurse that had been on duty the previous night and described the woman. He looked at me kind of funny and said he didn't know of anyone fitting that description, but he'd check for me. He did ask around, but there was no one on duty that could have been her. No CNAs, no respiratory therapists, or physical therapists, no one at all who matched her description. It was as if she simply didn't exist. I was frustrated and it seemed that no one believed my story.

That afternoon as we prepared to leave, my parents gathered my belongings, and I gathered my courage to brave the trip home. Slipping on my coat, I reached into my pockets for my gloves and felt something metal in my right pocket. I pulled it out and gasped. It was the black lab pin from my nurse's jacket. Now there was no question, she had been my Christmas angel.

DECEMBER 22

Every good gift and
every perfect gift is from above,
and cometh down from
the Father of lights.

James 1:17

At Christmas we are reminded of our bountiful blessings. There is always something we can be thankful for, and always someone who is going through a rougher patch than we are. Take time out of the hustle and bustle of today to experience the peace that comes from a thankful heart. Take a deep breath, get out a good book, and share a cup of hot chocolate or tea with a friend. Turn on the Christmas lights and music and just enjoy the moment. That is peace. It's not about your circumstances, it's about keeping your mind and your heart focused on what matters.

As a family, brainstorm names of people you can surprise this Christmas with a small gift. People that touch your life regularly, people that you might not think to give a gift to. For example, the mailman, the person who collects your trash, the lady at the convenience store where you get gas, the person at the grocery store who always helps you out with your groceries. How about the receptionist at the orthodontist's office or the janitor at your office or your child's school? All these people would be thrilled to be remembered at Christmas. Not something expensive, just thoughtful. A few cookies,a loaf of holiday bread, or a simple note would mean the world to them. It is a small thing you can do with a huge reward.

IT'S THE LITTLE THINGS

by Patricia Mitchell

One Christmas Eve, a princess looked out of her palace window, and she saw a boy selling chestnuts on the street corner below.

The boy wore a thin, tattered coat, a skimpy cap that barely covered his head, and old, torn mittens. Surely he was cold, the princess thought, yet he was singing as if he didn't have a care in the world. People had gathered around him, and many were buying his little bags of chestnuts.

Curious, the princess wrapped herself in her maid's plain and shabby cloak, and tiptoed out to join the crowd on the sidewalk. When the boy finished his song, the princess approached him and said, "My child, how cold you must be in a thin, tattered coat, a skimpy cap that barely covers your head, and those old, torn mittens!"

"It's true my clothes are not new, for I am only a poor boy who sells chestnuts. But I am glad and grateful, because people buy from me," the boy said to the princess. "Because they do, I can bring my mother and father and my brothers and sisters their very own orange to eat on Christmas Day. My good lady," he said to the princess, "would you like to buy my last little bag of chestnuts?"

"Why yes," the princess said, but her face fell when she realized she had no money with her. The boy quickly understood her predicament, and he held out his last little bag of chestnuts to her. "Please take this, Miss," he said. "I can see you're a poor girl, and I want you to have a gift to open on Christmas Day." Then the boy disappeared in the crowd, the strains of his merry carols dancing in the air like snowflakes.

The princess went back inside her palace. There, in a place of honor among all her many magnificent gifts, she tenderly set the little bag of chestnuts. It was the sweetest gift she had ever received—a gift that came from a humble and caring heart.

DECEMBER

23

Let every thing that hath breath praise the LORD. Praise ye the LORD.

Psalm 150:6

It's nearly Christmas Day. Everything seems to be decked out in red and green. Even the traffic lights are sporting the colors of the season! You have probably pulled boxes of decorations and ornaments up from the basement. Maybe you've gone to see the children in their play. There's a possibility you've finished your shopping by now. However, no matter what you may or may not have done this month, one thing is almost certain: you put up the Christmas tree! It is one of the most cherished Christmas traditions. Perhaps yours is a traditional tree you store away then get out every year. Or maybe you look and look for the perfect tree, tie it to the top of the car and take it home. You'll string it up with colorful lights, weigh it down with ornaments, place the best ornament on the very top, and secret packages wrapped in ribbons underneath. Turn down the lamps and admire the tree's magical transformation. It's beautiful. There is beauty all around us this season. What do you think is especially beautiful at Christmas?

Many of your ornaments may be symbols of the story of Jesus. How many of the following symbols are on your tree? An angel reminds us of the angels bringing the good news of His birth. A star symbolizes the Wise Men following the path to Jesus. Bells ring out the message of hope. A candy cane is shaped like the shepherd's staff, and turned upside down, it looks like the letter J for Jesus. Its colors stand for purity (white) and the blood that he shed for us (red). Prepare candy cane treats to give to others, either by hanging them on the tree or putting them on packages. Tie a bow around them, and attach a small note with a Christmas message.

DECEMBER 23

MY FAVORITE CHRISTMAS TREE

by Patricia Mitchell

That Christmas, I was living in a little London flat. Money wasn't plentiful, so I decided not to buy a tree or spend my precious pounds on ornaments and decorations. Yet after taking in all the bright lights and festive window displays throughout the city, I found my flat looking more and more forlorn.

A couple days before Christmas, I could stand it no longer. On a corner close to where I lived, I noticed that a shop had a few Christmas trees out on the sidewalk left to sell, so I went over to buy one. They were certainly scraggly specimens, but the price was right and I happily chose one and went back to my flat.

I stood the little tree in a bucket of sand and balanced it in the corner of my room, as I didn't have a real Christmas tree stand. Then I started to decorate.

For ornaments, I cut snowflakes out of folded paper, remembering the way we used to make these every year in grade school and how the teacher would hang them from the ceiling.

In the kitchen, I found a roll of aluminum foil. From it I cut sparkly silver slivers to hang over the tips of the tree's mostly bare branches. On the stronger branches of the tree, I placed Christmas cards I had received from family and friends (these proved especially good for covering empty spots, too).

Then I popped a bowl of popcorn, found a needle and thread, and strung a long garland that I draped around the increasingly satisfactory tree. On its tippy–top, I placed a star that I cut from the bottom of a pie pan.

I stood back to admire my work. The dangling foil strips caught the last low rays of a pale winter sun peeking from behind the clouds. The gentle light wreathed my little tree...my room...my heart in the warm glow of Christmas.

These days, my tall, full Christmas trees glitter with ornaments I've been collecting for years; but the little sparse "homemade" one in London remains my heart's most favorite tree.

DECEMBER 23

THE PERFECT CHRISTMAS

by Patricia Mitchell

One Christmas Eve, the stars shone bright
across the velvet nighttime sky.
Big lacy snowflakes softly fell
and wrapped my world in shimmered white.

"This is the perfect Christmas Eve!"
I said with pride...and yet...

Each ribboned gift, each shape and size,
was wrapped beneath my sparkling tree.
The candles glowed, the sweets set out
to welcome friends and family.

"This is the perfect Christmas Eve!"
I said with pride...and yet...

I looked around and there I found
that on the mantle shelf arrayed,
The manger scene with everything
except...except the Holy Babe!

In all the fuss that day and night,
in rushing in and dashing out,
I had forgotten that one thing
the celebration is about!

And so I found Him, laid Him there,
and knew whatever else might be,
When Jesus enters in each heart,
then it's the perfect Christmas Eve.

DECEMBER 24

...in thy presence is fullness of joy;
at thy right hand there are
pleasures for evermore.

Psalm 16:11

Christmas Eve at our church is always a display of contrasts. On the one hand, there is the childrens' nativity play which is usually fraught with mishaps and humor. What is more enjoyable than watching those sweet young faces clothed in shepherd's bathrobes and head towels or little wise men whose crowns that refuse to sit straight? Last year the four wise men and wise woman who were following the star appeared to lose their way when the star got stage-fright and led them right back from where they came. Luckily they found their way back and were able to present their gifts. One year Joseph and Mary fought over who got to hold the baby Jesus doll, and there was quite a commotion the year that one of the shepherds used his crook around a wise man's neck. I like to think that God smiles at our attempts to retell this amazing story.

Then there's the end of the service when we hear again the message of Jesus' birth. Our hearts well up with emotion as one-by-one, candles are lit, and voices join together for "Silent Night." We reflect on the gifts we've been given, and the hope that lies ahead in the New Year.

It's hard to find a more heart-blessed way of spending Christmas Eve than by going to a candlelight service. You may want to nap during the day so you can go to a midnight service. Afterward, you'll step into the night and Christmas Day will be here! Young children find that experience unforgettable. In some way today, be sure your family remembers the true story of Christmas from the Bible. It is printed on the back of your Advent calendar for you to read together. Now open window number 24!

CHARISSE
The Little Church Mouse

by Lauri Harper

My name is Charisse, and I am the official church mouse of the little Congregational Church in the little town of Middleton. I have lived in a cute little hole in the wall right behind the baptismal font for several years. I love my little church. We have a beautiful pipe organ, played every Sunday by Mrs. Lorsch. I always look forward to her Thursday afternoon practice time, but I do wish she would just play the organ and not try to sing. God gave her many gifts but singing was not one of them.

It was getting close to my favorite time of year in our little church, and that was Christmas. They decorate with live trees, holly, and berries so for a little mouse like me, it's a perfect time to get new bedding and things for my little hole in the wall next to the baptismal font. My favorite part of the entire Christmas service is when the children reenact the birth of Jesus. This year I thought we had the best cast of all for the Christmas play.

Our angel had the prettiest long golden locks of hair, Mary and Joseph made such a cute pair, and we even had a real baby to play Jesus! I was a little concerned though because the Pastor announced that this year they were adding a special treat to the Christmas play by having real animals as part of the play.

Christmas Eve finally arrived and Mrs. Lorsch was playing *Joy to the World* so loud, she nearly blew me right out of my house! I peered out behind the baptismal font and the entire church was full. Mary and Joseph were in place at the front of the church, with baby Jesus in the cradle. Our angelic angel stood next to the organ. I could feel butterflies in my stomach as I heard the song that was the cue for the rest of the cast to march down the aisle.

They had dimmed the lights and I could not figure out what was behind the three shepherd boys but it looked like it had ears! I just had to get a better look so I drew closer than I ever dared. I could hardly believe it when I saw it was a real donkey, followed by a llama, and two sheep! I was in such shock I didn't notice that the donkey had spotted me and we were now face-to-face. Well, what followed made church history. The donkey made a terrible noise and kicked the llama. The llama got so upset it spit right on the Pastor's wife! The lambs baaed, women screamed, babies cried—it was the worst noise ever heard in our little Congregational

Church. I ran as fast as my little legs would take me right up the pipe organ and onto Mrs. Lorsch's keyboard. I forgot that Mrs. Lorsch and I had never been formerly introduced, so as I ran across her fingers, she looked at me and gave a terrible gasp as her head hit the organ keys. The shepherds and their sheep were now blocking my little hole in the wall behind the baptismal font so I had no choice but to take a flying leap from the organ. I landed right on top of our angel's head! Everything suddenly got very quiet.

The Pastor made his way over to our beautiful angel where I was now trying to balance on her halo. He picked me up by my tail and for the first time in my entire life, I looked eye-to-eye with our Pastor. I saw out of the corner of my eye Mrs. Lorsch lifting her head up from the organ, but when she saw the Pastor holding me by my tail, she let out a scream that made the donkey kick, the llama spit and the sheep baa! The Pastor dropped me and I ran as fast as I could to my little hole in the wall behind the baptismal font.

That was the very last year they ever brought live animals into our little Congregational Church in the little town of Middleton and as the official church mouse, I couldn't be happier.

DECEMBER

25

For unto us a child is born…
and his name shall be called
Wonderful, Counsellor, The mighty God,
The everlasting Father,
The Prince of Peace.

Isaiah 9:6

Today is the day we've all been awaiting! It is finally time to open the 25th window on the Advent calendar, light the last candle on the Advent wreath, and honor the baby Jesus who now lays in the manger in the nativity scene. Today will be filled with fun and food, gifts and laughter. It's a time to treasure those we love. But most of all, it is a time to thank God for His greatest gift—Jesus our Savior. Our hopes turn toward the promises He holds in store for us, right around the corner in the New Year.

Enjoy this day, take time with each other, and give thanks to God for giving us the Christ child. As a family, take your time as you open your gifts to one another, don't just rush through. Focus on the blessing of being able to give. Start the exchange by having the youngest person choose one of the gifts he or she is giving to be the first opened. The recipient then can choose one of the gifts they are giving to be the next opened, and so forth. Finally, open the present for Jesus that you made on December 20. Remind each other of your promised gifts to Jesus. If you did not actually create a gift box, read that activity now and name aloud what each of you could give.

It is the day to celebrate the miracle that we have so been waiting for, the birth of precious Baby Jesus!

THE LEGEND OF THE BABY'S BREATH

By Doris Carter Wardlow

Long ago, there was a story told about shepherds guarding their sheep in Judean hills. Angels appeared to them and told them of a special baby, born in a manger in Bethlehem.

The angels gave their grand announcement to the excited shepherds, but standing on the outside of the circle was a curious little angel. The little one could not understand all the excitement but decided to go find out for herself.

The little angel found her way to the small town of Bethlehem and inquired how to find the stable and the special baby. Though it was very quiet, what an exciting scene it was! Shepherds were there and rich men too. Many animals had gathered about. As the angel moved closer she saw a man with calloused hands standing nearby and a dark-haired young lady looking with adoring eyes into the manger. She motioned for the angel to come closer and, standing on tiptoes, the little angel looked over the manger's edge.

At that moment, the baby's eyes opened and he smiled. The angel drew closer, and felt the breath of the

the sweet baby touch her face. As the angel made her way back up the hill, an amazing thing happened. With every step taken, tiny clusters of wispy white flowers began to bloom. One day, they would be known as baby's breath.

There are those who believe the lance-like leaves represent the pierced side, 33 years later, of the babe of Bethlehem, and the sweet white flower affirms the life of the good and pure man who taught us to love one another.

The Lord bless thee, and keep thee.

Numbers 6:24